MAY 1 8 2017

Who Stole Conservatism?

Who Stole Conservatism?

Capitalism and the Disappearance of Traditional Conservatism

Mario R. DiNunzio

 PRAEGER ™

An Imprint of ABC-CLIO, LLC
Santa Barbara, California • Denver, Colorado

Library of Congress Cataloging-in-Publication Data

Names: Di Nunzio, Mario R., 1936– author.
Title: Who stole conservatism? : capitalism and the disappearance of traditional
  conservatism / Mario R. DiNunzio.
Description: Santa Barbara, California : Praeger, an imprint of ABC-CLIO, LLC,
  2016. | Includes bibliographical references and index.
Identifiers: LCCN 2016010420 (print) | LCCN 2016010934 (ebook) |
  ISBN 9781440852824 (hardcopy : alk. paper) | ISBN 9781440852831 (ebook)
Subjects: LCSH: Conservatism—History. | Conservatism—
  United States—History.
Classification: LCC JC573 .D5 2016 (print) | LCC JC573 (ebook) |
  DDC 320.520973—dc23
LC record available at http://lccn.loc.gov/2016010420

ISBN: 978–1–4408–5282–4
EISBN: 978–1–4408–5283–1

20 19 18 17 16   1 2 3 4 5

This book is also available as an eBook.

Praeger
An Imprint of ABC-CLIO, LLC

ABC-CLIO, LLC
130 Cremona Drive, P.O. Box 1911
Santa Barbara, California 93116-1911
www.abc-clio.com

This book is printed on acid-free paper ∞

Manufactured in the United States of America

For Eli

Contents

Preface

There once was a time when conservatives and liberals could debate with vigor, taunt each other with wit, and govern together with honor for the general welfare as they understood it. That age now seems past.

This book is not an attack on either conservatism or capitalism. It is rather a lament for a lost conservatism the remnants of which have been distorted out of all recognition by a capitalism grasping for limitless power. Business world cunning has converted a conservatism that was once a voice of reasoned restraint into a shrill chorus in defense of a political program that erodes confidence in government and weakens democracy itself in order to discourage even the most modest action against the unrestrained pursuit of material gain. Political stagnation and legislative deadlock now pose a danger to the health of the American democracy. The intense individualism, libertarianism, and materialism of what passes for conservatism in the twenty-first century are not elements that fit any traditional understanding of conservatism. Those who cling to some remnant of traditional conservatism should be concerned about why and how the character of American conservatism shifted from its identification with transcendent values and cultural stability to an equation of individual freedom with material enterprise untroubled by concern for the common good. Such concern is rarely expressed in contemporary American conservative political discourse, and for that the republic is the poorer. The possibility of conservatives and liberals finding any minimal common ground seems to have disappeared from American politics, and the political process stagnates. If conservatives who long for the restoration of classic conservative ideals continue to support the libertarian conservatism that dominates contemporary American politics, genuine conservatism will become the dead relic of a dim past.

Introduction

The terms "conservative" and "liberal" are used differently in different contexts, and their precise meaning is often muddled. For example, writers in the nineteenth and early twentieth centuries often referred to the laissez-faire, free-enterprise economic theories usually associated with the ideas of Adam Smith as "liberal" economics. Some apply the term "conservative" both to the thought of Edmund Burke and to the ideas of libertarian Ayn Rand, but neither would have found compatibility or comfort in each other's company. Economist Friedrich von Hayek was not helpful when he asserted that he was not a conservative and then used the nineteenth-century application of "liberal" to sing the praises of free-enterprise capitalism. To help navigate the following chapters, a clarification of terms may serve.

In these pages, the terms "Burkean conservative," "classical conservative," or "traditional conservative" are applied to ideas and attitudes associated with founding conservative thinkers like Edmund Burke, and John Adams early on, and writers like Henry Adams, Richard Weaver, and Russell Kirk in the twentieth century. Despite inevitable variations among individuals, this kind of conservatism embraced a great respect for tradition, enduring moral values, and religion, and sustained skeptical attitudes toward popular, especially political, enthusiasms. Traditional or classic conservatism insisted not that novelty in society was bad in itself, but that core social, cultural, and political values should not be lightly sacrificed to passing fashion or self-interest. Community interest and community responsibility should reflect a society's traditions, religious and ethical values, cultural heritage, artistic legacy, concern for others, political programs, and economic life. Change could be embraced, but ought not to do damage. This conservatism intended to serve stability, order, organic development, and the common good without risking the perils of uncontrolled and unpredictable social upheaval.

This interpretation of conservatism must be distinguished from the American conservative movement that emerged during the post–Civil War Gilded Age and that directed its energies to a defense of capitalism even at the cost of muting, altering, or even abandoning important ideas of classical conservatism. Modern conservatism in America since the Gilded Age has included an amalgam of sometimes incompatible ideas about politics, culture, and morality, but it has been dominated, it is argued here, by its blind support for unregulated business enterprise. In the modern world, at least since the second half of the nineteenth century, capitalism has become a dominant influence for change in society with little regard for preservation or continuity and much distortion of culture and values. Libertarians are often welcomed to the work of conservative causes and many of them embrace the conservative label. But libertarians, at base, wish the function of government to be effectively limited to defense against violent crime and foreign enemies with few, if any, restraints on individual social or economic behavior. They are, in fact, far from conservative by any useful definition. The pernicious influence of the capitalist and the libertarian has transformed traditional conservatism beyond recognition.

Liberalism here is applied to those ideas and movements often called "progressive" and associated with Theodore Roosevelt, Woodrow Wilson, Franklin Roosevelt, and a roster of twentieth-century leaders like Harry Truman, the three Kennedy brothers, Martin Luther King, Hubert Humphrey, and others. Their liberalism regarded government action as an essential tool in the work of economic and social justice and believed that a regulated capitalism should be made to serve the commonweal. While liberals often differ on specific policies, especially on social issues in recent decades, their progressive agenda has been more clear and coherent than the confusions that have plagued the modern American conservative movement for over a century.

Traditional conservatism and liberalism rooted in Jeffersonian idealism, the Social Gospel of the Progressive Era, and the reforms of the New Deal are significantly different, but they are not complete opposites. They propose differences of pace; their priorities bear different emphases; their understandings of human nature and human potential clash. But in the full context of American history, both conservatives and liberals sustained a commitment to the ideals of the Founders, best expressed in the Declaration of Independence. It is interesting that both looked to Jefferson for inspiration: liberals for his embrace of change, his egalitarianism, and his faith in democracy and the common man; conservatives for his distrust of a too strong central government and his emphasis on the free individual. Hard-fought and confusing clashes followed during the first half of the nineteenth century that do not seem to fit more recent understanding of the words "conservative" and "liberal." For example, a conservative John Quincy Adams proposed national university and a federally sponsored program of public works; the Jeffersonians of the Jacksonian era demurred. A conservative John Calhoun, a fiery nationalist as a young man, later defended the rights of the states against federal authority in order to preserve human slavery. A liberal Andrew Jackson, heir to the Jeffersonian Democratic Party, quashed the nullification movement in South Carolina, and, in the process, he strengthened the presidency and the national government. Liberals favored the elimination of property qualifications for voting; conservatives thought property inclined the electorate toward more responsible and cautious government. There were indeed differences between American liberal and conservative forces in the early nineteenth century, but the context of those disputes was very different from those in the twentieth century, and the labels do not translate easily from one century to another. Sectional issues, above all questions concerning slavery, made sharp definitions difficult. Both liberals and conservatives were committed to the ideals of democratic experiment. Disagreements came in judging the best course and the proper pace of change toward the fulfillment of those ideals. Liberals were more open to ideas of political and social reform and optimistic about the possibilities of positive change in human behavior and in the improvement of society. American conservatives shared with their European counterparts a reverence for tradition, a respect for order, a suspicion of popular enthusiasms and utopian promises, and subscribed to a darker vision of human nature.

With the rise of super-powerful industrial and finance capitalism in the second half of the century, something happened to traditional conservatism that changed its character and dramatically altered the debate between those who called themselves conservative and those who embraced the label liberal. The new capitalism identified itself with and dominated conservative discourse, refocused conservative purpose, and has ever since harnessed conservatism to the indiscriminate service of business enterprise. Capitalism stole conservatism and holds it captive without apology.

~~~

The words "conservative" and "liberal" came into common use in the political jargon of the Western world in the years after the French Revolution and largely in reaction to it. Many European liberals looked to the success of the democratic experiment in the United States rather than the French Revolution. In France, what began with hope-filled steps toward a constitutional monarchy, an end to the medieval special privileges of the aristocracy, and the chartering of civil liberties devolved into the Terror of Robespierre and rigid dictatorships under the Directory and Napoleon. Liberals did, however, champion some of the ideals broadcast but never fulfilled by the French Revolution. The slogan was French, but it was Americans who moved steadily toward expanded liberty, equality, and fraternity. Throughout the nineteenth century, European reformers invoked the American experience to defend their demands for civil and political liberty. From London to St. Petersburg, liberals and even radicals pointed to the Americans to inspire their own struggles for reform.

The French Revolution horrified conservatives not only because of its barbaric excesses but because the French had deemed revolution necessary at all. Their commitment to and defense of monarchy excused the failures and outrages of the Old Regime in France. Even when they acknowledged some of those failures in retrospect, conservatives insisted that the character of the French revolutionary response was extreme and unwarranted. The result, they believed, was not reform but disaster. They saw the years from 1789 through the Napoleonic era as destructive of tradition, religion, good order, and stable political and social structures. The Revolution in France set off a quarter century of political upheaval, repression, and war. Regicide, Jacobin terror, dictatorship, and Napoleonic megalomania destroyed too much and improved too little.

The final defeat of Napoleon and the agreements reached at the Congress of Vienna in 1815 ushered in an era of reaction and continued repression marked by a panicky fear of both reform and revolution, a fear that recognized little distinction between the two. Elsewhere, Clement von Metternich of Austria dominated the Congress of Vienna, and his influence shaped the decades that followed. Agreements at Vienna led the French restore the Bourbon monarchy under Louis XVIII and his more intensely oppressive successor Charles X. Metternich also supported repressive regimes across Europe that imposed censorship, crushed student groups, and regarded any proposal for reform as a prelude to another revolution. None of this could stifle the urge for reform, especially when repression took place in full view of the success of the American democratic experiment with its expanding franchise, unprecedented individual freedom, and growing prosperity. Apologies to Marx, it was the specter of *democracy* that haunted Europe.

Outbursts of reform protests, an unproductive revolt in France under Louis Phillipe in 1830, and fruitless uprisings throughout Europe in 1848 settled little but exposed a continuing instability born of the French Revolution. These troubles only confirmed the governing prejudice that repression was essential to avoid disaster. The more intensely offended abhorred anything that suggested an adjustment to modern ideas. The major ruling houses of Europe hoped for the collapse of the American experiment; they understood the powerful inspiration reformers drew from America. The discomfort of Europe's elites with American democracy persisted past mid-century, and they hoped to label the American experiment a failure. With the ironic exception of Russia, the major powers of Europe hoped for a Southern victory in the American Civil War, and Britain and France endowed the Confederacy with substantial material aid. Democracy was simply not yet acceptable to the traumatized conservatives of Europe.

Some more sensitive conservatives understood that total and blind resistance to change was neither wise nor practical. However, political and social change, if any be entertained, should be gradual, organic, and compatible with tradition and established institutions. There could be no genuine liberty without order, and governments should be strong enough to maintain order and certainly strong enough to stifle social upheaval. Conservatives understood human nature to be flawed, prone to mischief or worse, and in need of restraint. This was especially true for the untutored masses. Conservatives doubted those notions of the goodness of man born of Enlightenment and Romantic optimism as well as the supposed wisdom of the majority. Good order dictated a stratified social structure and the protection of property, which they saw as an essential support for stability. The propertied they earnestly argued, those with the greatest stake in an ordered society, should rule. To sustain good order and a stable society, conservatives favored a tempered individualism mindful of the civic responsibilities of elite leadership.

Liberals, on the other hand, welcomed change and questioned the engrained institutions and customs of Europe, many of which were rooted in and reflective of the conditions of a medieval world long dead. The liberal outlook was complex. It looked for broader popular participation in government, though European middle class liberals, in a spasm of sympathy with conservatives, proved reluctant for some time to extend the franchise to the working class. After all, working class demands would certainly require increased taxation of the middle and upper classes, the working class having precious little income to tax. During the risings of 1848, the temporarily victorious middle classes called out the military to check the demands of the workers who had helped make possible the early success of those revolutions. An angry and alienated working class, shut out of participation in reform, turned to the more radical appeal of Marxist ideas of economic determinism that neither conservatives nor liberals could abide. Liberals leaned toward republican constitutional forms incompatible with aristocracy and autocratic monarchy. Heavily influenced by both Enlightenment and Romantic thought, they saw human nature as benign and reformable when it was not benign. They placed greater confidence in the notion that education and an improved social environment could reduce crime, poverty, and antisocial behavior generally. Though not levelers, liberals tended to combine the hope for liberty with a commitment to civic equality. American examples were important. Freedom of religion, separation of church and state, free speech and press, and a broadening suffrage proved irresistibly attractive models for liberals in a postrevolutionary Europe of continuing repression.

Unlike their twentieth-century heirs, liberals in the nineteenth century warmly supported laissez-faire economics and were deeply suspicious of government power, given the history of atrocities by authoritarian governments. Liberals admired the economic ideas of Adam Smith, which provided an alternative to the regnant policies of mercantilism, a practice of heavily detailed supervision of economic activity by government. For some centuries mercantilism had been the prevailing practice of all the major European powers who believed that economic success supported military success, and therefore, economics was too important to be left to the private ambitions of businessmen. Smith's theory that everyone, governments, businessmen, and the public would be better served by free enterprise appealed to liberals who already harbored deep suspicion of and hostility toward overbearing governments. The appeal of Smith to liberals contributed to the confusion of labels that must always be considered in their temporal contexts. The economic ideas associated with Adam Smith took on the labels "liberal" or "classical" economics, designations that persisted into the early twentieth century. The creed of "liberal economics" embraced ideas like "the invisible hand," the magical effects of supply and demand, and the natural and inevitable self-correction of the market left to itself. The labels changed even as the ideas persisted.

Conservatives and liberals have fought fierce political battles over the years, and in the heat generated by partisanship they have described each other with intense prejudice. Liberal slurs of conservatives have ranged from "elitist snobs" to "fascists." Conservatives have assaulted liberals with a list of libels from the rather gentle "naive dreamers" to "crypto-Marxists schemers for a classless society." Hyperbole might add some spice to political debate, but their real differences are not so acute. Liberalism and conservatism in the nineteenth century were different from each other, but they were not absolute opposites. At least some of the differences were matters of pace. Genuine liberals did not intend the complete destruction of traditional institutions, but they were quicker to identify the need for change and less fearful of modernization. For liberals too much tradition and too many outdated institutions were remnants of a feudal era that could not endure in an age of industrialism and urbanization. They demanded adaptations to the new social and political realities resulting from the rise of a larger middle class and a new working class. They saw that the world had changed, and old formulas and old rules demanded revision to cope with new conditions. Some conservatives, especially men like Edmund Burke, conceded the need for and, on occasion, actively campaigned for modest reforms in the service of stability. Reactionaries fearfully resisted all the changes dictated by modern conditions, but many conservatives recognized the wisdom of Burke.

The United States produced its quota of conservatives who shared many of the concerns of their European counterparts. But in America there was more sympathy for republican government from the start, even if there were serious concerns about the leveling influence of intensifying democratic practice. Most Americans believed their own revolutionary propaganda, and they developed a powerful sense of mission to serve as a guiding beacon for the reformers of the old world. Most conservatives in America were more sympathetic to republican ideals than their European brothers. American conservatives valued liberty over equality; liberals tended to cheer for both. Liberals and conservatives in America were committed to individualism, property rights, community responsibility, and effective government. Their disagreements rose out of the details, the timing, and the presumed consequences of particular policies. Americans argued about the power of government, but the shape of the argument does not neatly fit the current conceptions of liberal and conservative.

In the nineteenth century, conservatives admired effective government; it was liberals who were wary of government power.

In the early republic the father of the American liberal tradition was Thomas Jefferson, while conservatives looked to John Adams and his Federalist allies. Jefferson was a child of the Enlightenment. His felicitous language of equality and liberty in the Declaration of Independence shook the world, and its inspiration endures. He expressed a great faith in the common man, insisted on the need for the protection of civil liberties, and embraced the ideals of democracy with an undisguised fervor. Although always open to the possibilities of change, he was, nevertheless, oddly conservative in his suspicion of the rapid advance of industry. He dreamed, rather, of an agrarian America of yeoman farmers jealous of their freedom who would serve as guarantors of a continuing democracy. Having lived free and extracted a living from the soil by his own hard work, the American farmer, Jefferson thought, would be most resistant to any assaults on democratic liberties. In his European travels he associated the oppression he saw with authoritarian monarchies and the poverty he witnessed with the new and expanding factory system. He hoped America could avoid these conditions. For the American experiment, he insisted on a constitutional philosophy that embraced republicanism, and he sustained a lively suspicion that some American leaders preferred the British model of government, including its elitism and its monarchy. While he favored a federal government strong enough to be stable, he also believed governing power should remain as close as possible to those governed—in the states. Jefferson generally supported a narrow interpretation of the constitutional powers of the federal government. His was the liberal stance in the age of the early republic.

The more conservative voices of Alexander Hamilton and the elder and younger Adams presidents called out for stronger and more active governments to maintain order in society and to actively stimulate internal improvements and economic growth. These conservative minds embraced the American democratic experiment, but they feared that too much democracy, too much political authority in the hands of the un-propertied, too little government power would destroy the experiment and generate chaos.

By the end of the nineteenth century, liberals and conservatives would trade some of these ideas about government, contributing to more confusion in the use of the terms. Liberals began to look for federal government action for economic and social justice; conservatives began to see the power of federal government as a problem. Thus, liberal and conservative approaches to government as well as their economic prejudices must be understood in the context of history.

As their attitudes changed, so did the meaning of the labels. Some postures remained consistent regardless of the timing. Liberals remained more open to innovation and less patient with tradition. Conservatives were steady in their insistence of good order, prudent development, and enduring cultural and moral values.

Thus, in the postrevolutionary era the ideological lines were drawn, and conservative thinkers explicated and refined a philosophy of politics, society, and culture designed to defend against the rapid, impromptu, and unanchored changes modernity visited on the West. While differing conditions dictated some variations in thought among Europeans and Americans, conservatives generally agreed in their emphasis on stability, respect for tradition, suspicion of the volatile masses and the need for authoritative, if not authoritarian, government. Rejecting a pure materialism, conservatives saw the importance of the spiritual values in human affairs. On both sides of the Atlantic, conservatives nurtured a great respect for, if not always, a dedicated commitment to religion, even if some of their number challenged religious orthodoxy. A stable moral order inspired by traditional religious values was as important as, and a prerequisite for, a stable social order.

~~~

Conservatism as a political ideology is not what it used to be or what it was originally intended to be. Conservatism as now expressed in American political culture little resembles the collection of ideas crafted by Edmund Burke, John Adams, and other political thinkers in defense of a stable and secure society in the aftermath of the French Revolution. Indeed, contemporary conservatism undermines key elements in the architecture of classic conservative theory. The distortion of conservative thought as applied to politics has become so grotesque that what now passes for conservatism would have appalled its founding apostles. The principal culprit in this transformation is an idealized capitalism that feeds a pervasive materialism. The consequences for society cannot be reconciled with and are, in fact, inimical to the founding philosophy of conservatism. Beginning in the late nineteenth century, the more intense practitioners and guardians of capitalist enterprise seduced, captivated, and converted avowed conservatives by forging and twisting elements of conservative ideology into a steely defense of unrestrained business enterprise. What has passed for conservative political thought ever since is so intimately wedded to the pecuniary objectives of corporate capital that it has lost any genuine claim to the longstanding tradition of reasoned, classic conservatism. Tainted by the capitalist distortions, conservative political thought has become thoroughly materialist, perversely individualist, and narrowly focused on adjusting all political and economic policy to serve the manipulators of capital.

Contemporary conservatism is now so closely tied to the uncritical defense of capitalist free enterprise that conservative discourse shows little concern for the differences between wealth accumulation and the pernicious social consequences of undisciplined enterprise. Thus, public squalor, urban and rural, draws little conservative editorial or political outrage, but taxes and government expenditures are assaulted as intolerable evils. Meanwhile, ostentatious private opulence proudly glitters, untroubled by the obligations of civic responsibility. Legislative efforts toward insuring access to health care or establishing an economic safety net of security for the neediest in society are dismissed as profligate public expenditure on behalf of the undeserving.

This critique is not intended as an attack on capitalism as an economic system per se. Capitalism has been massively productive and has clearly raised the standard of living of millions, though not without huge cost in human suffering. Historically, conservatives and liberals both committed themselves to the political and ideological support of capitalism as an economic system. However, the development of a blind devotion of capitalists during the Gilded Age to uncontrolled, free-market economic practice with little regard for consequences made capitalism a system whose brutality was impossible to disguise. The new industrial/finance capitalism of the age demanded rationalization, and its apologists sought and found both religious and pseudo-scientific justifications for its legitimacy. In building arguments for that justification, capitalists bred mutations in conservative ideas and reassembled them to defend their dominant influence on the nation's economics and politics. In the next century the obsession of the West with the very real dangers of an aggressive Communism no doubt contributed to the virtual sanctification of capitalism by conservatives, especially in its laissez-faire incarnation. Any alternative to absolute free enterprise was regarded simply as a step toward socialism and slavery. Those who proposed some restraints on the indiscriminate and irresponsible power of capital, like the two presidents Roosevelt, conservatives labeled dangerous fools or traitors. Among most Americans the devotion to laissez-faire have endured, sparking doubts only briefly in times of economic crisis, and among the most determined conservatives, not even then. The evident success of mixed economies without the destruction of individual freedom or democratic practice, for example in Scandinavian countries and to a lesser extent in the rest of Europe, has simply been ignored. Since the late nineteenth century, American conservatives have described any government interference with free capitalist enterprise as a prescription for inevitable economic and political disaster.

The right of an undiscriminating capitalism to invest in virtually any enterprise, however sordid or socially damaging, without interference or oversight by public authority, has been weirdly defended as essential to the survival of human freedom. Enabling quasi-pornographic publications to become legitimate media enterprises listed on the stock exchange drew no expression of dismay from conservatives who professed high moral standards. Conservatives have mounted no campaigns to protest the sleaziness of so much advertising or the constant drumbeat to stimulate consumerism. The modern American conservative offers impassioned support for the unchallenged right to buy arms without limit, resisting even checks against felons or the mentally unstable at fly-by-night gun shows, and does not object to even the most limited restraints on the killing power of high-caliber assault weaponry. Witness decades of virtually blind support for military expenditure and the blending of genuine patriotic support for the troops at risk with a blank check for the military/industrial complex. Perhaps it was President Eisenhower's warning about this that inspired the more avid on the right to accuse him of Communist sympathy. How rare it has been for conservative leaders or the rank and file to find a military adventure they did not support without question. The sum of these parts composes a portrait of modern American conservatism fully out of touch with its roots. In this picture one cannot recognize the reasoned social and political worldview that informed the conservatism of Edmund Burke or John Adams and his generation.

In the decades after the French Revolution, American conservatives shaped a creed hostile to rapid and careless innovations, and they hoped to preserve what they thought to be the best Western traditions in a society of stability and sound reason. It was a temperate ideology with some variations among its advocates, some of the more intense of whom could be tempted to reaction. Conservatives remained open to change, but resisted the hyperactive imaginings of those they deemed naïve, if not dangerous, liberals. The preachers of that faith established a conservative tradition in the nineteenth century that was eventually assaulted and altered not by liberal enemies but by other self-proclaimed conservatives who distorted the creed beyond recognition, but continued to apply the label to very unconservative thought and action. Many faithful conservatives clung to the orthodox ideas of responsible and stable governments presiding over a society committed to rational change, respectable values, and cultural sophistication. But others who called themselves conservatives appended new ideas and purpose to drive conservatism into the service of capitalist enterprise. The result was a perverse and adulterated rendition of conservatism. The purer original conservative faith became an interesting antique of limited utility in the new world of finance capitalism and mega-industry. The ensuing struggle to define the soul of conservatism was won by a new class of enthusiasts who welded conservative ideas so closely to unfettered capitalism that classic conservatism was rendered impotent to counter an increasingly individualist and materialist modernity. By the twenty-first century what passes for conservatism would have astounded the founders. Contemporary conservatism has not only abandoned important tenets of the original conservative formula but has also embraced ideas and public policies that undermine the very heart of the ideology. The label survives; the essence is grossly distorted. The following chapters will examine the process by which capitalists stole conservatism and still hold it captive.

Architects of Classic Conservatism

The most celebrated founding voice of conservative thought was that of Edmund Burke.

Burke was born in Dublin, Ireland, in 1729, but he always considered himself an Englishman. Though his mother was a Catholic, he embraced the Anglicanism of his father's side of the family and was educated in Anglican tradition at Trinity University. After taking his degree there, he moved to London to prepare for a career in the law. Burke sustained the same confidence in the power of reason as did many of his Enlightenment contemporaries, but while the intellectual fashion of the day led many of them toward a unitarian Deism, he remained a devout Christian. He built a reputation in London circles as a writer of well-reasoned and powerfully written essays and soon entered the world of politics. In 1756 he became secretary to the future prime minister, the Marquis of Rockingham, opening a path to the highest levels of British politics. Burke continued as a friend and advisor to Rockingham for many years. He himself entered Parliament in 1766, serving for almost 30 years until 1794 as one of its most respected members.

Burke is the exemplar of a conservative who could also advocate and support reform without apology or embarrassment. Some of his earliest speeches in Parliament concerned events in America. After the great and very expensive victory over the French in the Seven Years' War, the British government decided to tighten controls over its colonies with an eye toward increasing revenues. New trade regulations and especially the passage of the Stamp Act in 1865 sparked tensions between the colonies and the mother country that only grew worse. The American colonists saw these acts as novel and unwelcome intrusions on their prerogatives. Burke recognized the legitimacy of colonial grievances, and he understood what his colleagues in Britain could not fathom: that the Americans had by that time developed an effective machinery of self-government even while remaining loyal to the king. Given the worsening tensions that followed the Stamp Act and other duties London imposed on the colonies, good relations required careful thought beyond the simplistic ideas that treated the American entities as mere possessions. These were not one-crop, money machines like the sugar islands; the 13 continental colonies had grown into complex societies of diverse populations and politics. This Burke understood. In 1775 he published a version of a speech he delivered in Parliament entitled *Conciliation with America.* He doubted the efficacy of tighter controls from London and argued for some accommodation toward a measure of colonial autonomy within a united empire. Anticipating the idea of a British Commonwealth arrangement, his was thinking in advance of its age, too far advanced for the less-flexible minds in Parliament and in the monarchy of George III.

When repeated disputes led to military conflict, Burke, still hoping for reconciliation, referred not to "revolution" but to the "American war." He assigned its cause to bad management by a stiff-necked government and continued to hope for the recognition of a significant measure of American freedom and self-government without full independence. He looked toward a kind of federalism. Though Burke continued to push the case for conciliation, the tides of war swept Americans away from any enduring link to Britain. He finally acknowledged that preserving a healthy and lasting connection with the united colonists demanded changes and concessions that neither Parliament nor Crown could abide. Then, and repeatedly later, Burke understood that to conserve required innovation and risk.

Edmund Burke also lobbied for the correction of the injustices in the British governance of India. A persistent critic of the East India Company for its abuses and corruption in the management of Indian affairs, Burke awakened public attention to the suffering of the people of India. He published essays and spoke in Parliament about the importance of morality and duty in the conduct of imperial governance, with special concern for the welfare of those governed. He pleaded to a largely unresponsive audience in an age when relaxed notions of conflict of interest carried substantial profits to members of Parliament, the government, and even the royal family.

Critical of official discrimination in Britain, Burke supported extending civil liberties to Roman Catholics and religious dissenters. The abuses of British rule in Ireland earned his scorn, and there, too, he proposed concessions and conciliation. He also joined reformers calling for an end to the slave trade in the empire, and, unlike many of the conservatives of his day, he was a Whig, not a Tory, despite his enduring respect for the monarchy. Clearly, here was a man of imaginative and flexible political disposition, a man of conservative instincts convinced that sustaining a healthy and stable empire required innovative, temperate, and sensitive governing policies. It was not obvious from his support for a variety of political causes that Burke would become a founding voice of traditional conservatism.

It was Burke's comments on the French Revolution that more than anything else made him a paragon of conservative thought. His most famous work, *Reflections on the Revolution in France*, stands an inaugural moment for modern conservative political philosophy. In the earliest stages of the uprising in France, he recognized disaster in the making even at a time when most of the changes wrought by the Revolution could be considered moderate, especially when compared to what happened later during the years of the Terror and the Directory. Burke published the book early in November 1790, and before the month was out a French translation was being sold in Paris. The book was an instant best seller in both countries. Burke found an eager audience among those worried about where the Revolution in France might lead. In England the book sold over 10,000 copies within the first month of publication, and in only a few months the French version alone sold over 15,000 copies. These were remarkable numbers in publishing for that era, and indeed would delight most authors today.

The first year of the Revolution established what amounted to a constitutional monarchy in France. A new charter crafted by the National Assembly certainly diminished the king's authority, but he remained the head of state and retained significant veto powers over legislation. The revolutionaries confiscated church lands to pay for the endemic and catastrophic debt the French government had accrued over past decades, but such confiscation was not unprecedented among European monarchies in the eighteenth century. Across Europe, even in devoutly Christian countries, monarchs fully committed to the faith of their national churches took steps to increase their authority over church matters. Rulers removed education from church control and made it a function of the state. They sold monastic lands and other formerly church-controlled properties to feed the coffers of the state. In France the church was exempt from taxation, and repeatedly during the prerevolutionary economic crisis, churchmen had, along with the nobility, refused to approve legislation for even the most moderate imposition of taxes.

Unpleasant as they were for the regime, one could read the events of those first months of the French Revolution as an attempt to catch up with political changes already in place elsewhere in Europe. It might be plausibly compared to the ascendancy of Parliament during the British Revolution of 1688–1689. This was not an entirely unreasonable interpretation of the first year of the revolt in France. Burke would have none of it. In 1688–1689 the British deposed a king, James II, and Parliament installed new monarchs, William of Orange and Mary, the Protestant daughter of Catholic James. The Parliament also worked substantial changes in the British constitution. These were not small events. But Burke defended that revolt as rooted in British tradition and constitutional limits. It was, he argued, the overthrow of a monarch, not a monarchy.

> The two principles of conservation and correction operated strongly at the two critical periods of the Restoration and Revolution, when England found herself without a king. At both those periods the nation had lost the bond of union in their ancient edifice; they did not, however dissolve the whole fabric. On the contrary, in both cases they regenerated the deficient part of the old constitution through the parts which were not impaired. . . . At no time, perhaps, did the sovereign legislature manifest a more tender regard to that fundamental principle of British constitutional policy, than at the time of the Revolution, when it deviated from the direct line of hereditary succession. The Crown was carried somewhat out of the line in which it had before moved; but the new line was derived from the same stock. It was still a line of hereditary descent; still an hereditary descent in the same blood, though an hereditary descent qualified with protestantism [*sic*]. When the legislature altered the direction, but kept the principle, they showed that they held it inviolable.[1]

One might well argue that Burke offered a somewhat strained and rather benign reading of the British Revolution of 1688–1689, which its partisans liked to call the "Glorious Revolution." Though King James II, unlike Louis XVI, escaped to live in exile, he *was* dethroned, constitutional change significantly limited the power of the monarchy, religious hatred was a strong motivating force, and the resulting parliamentary supremacy broke with British tradition. But Burke insisted the English Revolution did not overturn a social order as did the French, but rather it restored a more just social balance that had been distorted by the Stuart monarchs. Burke had offended some of his contemporaries of conservative inclination by his sympathy for the American cause despite the dramatically radical character, for its time, of the emerging popular democracy. He saw no contradictions here. He interpreted both the American and the English Revolutions as restrained movements toward order and stability; they did not offend his conservative temper.

The revolt in 1688, then, restored ancient rights that had been damaged by James II and was thus defensive and conservative in character, according to Burke. Not so in France. The king, Burke thought, had been rendered impotent. The rebels unjustly confiscated royal and church lands to benefit themselves and investors who bought the properties at modest cost and who were supportive of the Revolution. Too much had changed too rapidly with insufficient respect for traditional institutions and customs. Burke was convinced that what was happening in France was not reform but the destruction of basic foundations of the society. He insisted that the leaders of National Assembly usurped power without precedent or warrant and far exceeded the wishes of the people who elected them. The people chose them to reform the government, but they set out to destroy it. "The improvements of the national assembly are superficial, their errors fundamental." Attacks on the church amounted, it seemed to him, to an attempt to destroy Christianity. Indeed, that became the announced policy of the Jacobins during the Reign of Terror, when they converted churches into temples dedicated to Reason and replaced statues of the saints with casts of Voltaire and Rousseau. (Revolutionaries tend to be very serious people, but they cannot always avoid the comic.) Burke predicted that France would soon be governed by an "ignoble oligarchy, founded on the destruction of the crown, the church, the nobility, and the people," and he missed only the last leap of the Revolution into Napoleonic dictatorship.[2]

In *Reflections* Burke also launched an attack on French leaders of the Enlightenment, who had inspired so much modern innovation and challenged so much of tradition with excessive zeal and hidden agendas. Without naming names, but with reference to the contributors to the *Encyclopedie* of Diderot, he referred to gentlemen who "stood high in the ranks of literature and science." He would no doubt have had Diderot, Voltaire, and Rousseau in mind when he attributed to "These Atheistical fathers . . . a bigotry of their own." They were, he thought, a "literary cabal" planning "the destruction of the Christian religion." "These writers . . . pretended to a great zeal for the poor, and the lower orders, whilst in their satires they rendered hateful, by every exaggeration, the faults of courts, of nobility, and of priesthood. [No doubt a slam at Voltaire.] They became a sort of demagogues." He was especially hostile to the ideas of Jean Jacques Rousseau and accounted him a principal inspiration for the French Revolution. While some Enlightenment thinkers remained faithful Christians, Burke was not far off the mark in attacking those iconoclasts among the philosophes who sanctified empirical reason, equated faith with superstition, and aimed at annihilating both. For him the French Revolution was extreme, not aiming simply at the overthrow of a particular political order, but dedicated to the thorough remaking of the political, social, religious, and cultural life of the society. What collection of men could be so wise as to complete such a project with beneficent results?[3]

Burke had little patience for the leveling rhetoric of the revolutionaries. "Believe me, Sir, those who attempt to level, never equalize." "The levelers therefore only change and pervert the natural order of things." The idea that persons of low standing should be deemed qualified to govern he rejected, echoing the conservative prejudice of the age. "The occupation of hair-dresser, or of a working tallow-chandler, cannot be a matter of honour to any person—to say nothing of a number of more servile employments. Such descriptions of men ought not to suffer oppression from the state; but the state suffers oppression, if such as they, either individually or collectively are permitted to rule." The responsibilities of government should be entrusted to those better capable of handling them: the propertied and the well born. Some preference given to birth "is neither unnatural, nor unjust, nor impolitic." "As to the people [of France] at large, when once these miserable sheep have broken the fold, and have got themselves loose, not from the restraint, but from the protection of all the principles of natural authority, and legitimate subordination, they became the natural prey of impostors."[4]

Such ideas may seem quaintly antique, but in Europe they were part of the conservative conviction of that era that the masses had neither the education nor the sophistication required for responsible participation in government. This remained a conservative conviction through much of the nineteenth century and into the twentieth. For some conservatives, wealth, however accumulated, testified to wisdom and intellectual strength. In Europe there was little doubt that broad participation in the political life of a nation could only mean trouble. Perhaps the American experience was still too young to impress even as it moved very early toward a broadening franchise. Even in America the movement for universal (white, male) suffrage after the Revolution was not universally applauded, nor have misgivings about the qualifications of the working poor to vote entirely disappeared. Echoes of these ideas remain a prejudice still entertained in some of the more radically conservative circles today, as efforts to restrict access to the polls testify.

Burke was not averse to reform as his past record clearly suggested, but he believed change must improve and not destroy established institutions. To reform and simultaneously preserve is a delicate process that, when properly done, moves exceedingly slowly. A slow pace is cautious, and caution is necessary for successful change. "By a slow but well sustained progress, the effect of each step is watched; the good or ill success of the first gives light to us in the second; and so from light to light, we are conducted with safety through the whole series." His was a conservative vision of organic change.[5]

Burke's conservatism was rooted in his understanding of natural law. In *Reflections* he refers to "the great primaeval contract of eternal society, linking the lower with the higher natures, connecting the visible and invisible world, according to a fixed compact sanctioned by the inviolable oath which holds all physical and moral natures, each to their appointed place." "He who gave our nature to be perfected by our virtue, willed also the necessary means of its perfection— He willed therefore the state."[6] There was, then, a divine sanction for both good order and liberty guided by natural law; it should not be easily tampered with by men.

For Burke, history and tradition were critically important for the stability of a society.

> You will observe, from the Magna Charta to the Declaration of Right, it has been the uniform policy of our constitution to claim and assert our liberties, as an *entailed inheritance* derived to us from our forefathers, and to be transmitted to our posterity. . . . By this means our constitution preserves as unity in so great a diversity of its parts. We have an inheritable crown; and inheriting peerage; and an house of commons and a people inheriting privileges, franchises, and liberties, from a long line of ancestors.
>
> This policy appears to me to be the result of profound reflection; or rather the happy effect of following nature, which is wisdom without reflection, and above it. A spirit of innovation is generally the result of a selfish temper and confined views. People will not look forward to posterity, who never look backward to their ancestors.[7]

Another bulwark of a stable society, for Burke, was the influence of religion, which he called "the source of all good and of all comfort." He was profoundly distressed by the attacks on religion in France.

> We know, and it is our pride to know, that man is by his constitution a religious animal; that atheism is against, not only our reason but our instincts; and that it cannot prevail long. But if, in the moment of riot, and in a drunken delirium from the hot spirit drawn out of the alembick of hell, which in France is now so furiously boiling, we should uncover our nakedness by throwing off the Christian religion which has hitherto been our boast and comfort, and one great source of civilization among us, and among other nations, we are apprehensive (being well aware that the mind will not endure a void) that some uncouth, pernicious, and degrading superstition, might take place of it.[8]

Burke looked for a balance among liberty, individualism, and the common good and sought to define the liberty he believed all were entitled to. "The Liberty I mean is *social* freedom. It is that state of things in which Liberty is secured by the equality of Restraint; a Constitution of things in which the Liberty of no one Man, and no body of Men and no Number of Men can find means to trespass on the Liberty of any Person or any description of persons in the Society. This kind of Liberty is indeed but another name for Justice, ascertained by wise Laws and secured by well-constructed institutions."[9] He would have judged public policy directed merely to serve the material interests of an individual or a private group as unjust and an unworthy of good government.

In *Reflections on the Revolution in France*, Burke broadcast ideas he had been cultivating for a lifetime, and the book stood as a statement of conservative principles in support of tradition, hierarchy, gradual change, and respect for religion, order, and stability. Burke believed in a God-given natural law embedded in the hearts and minds of all, which formed the basic principles for governing social and political life. Though not all conservatives were theists, they broadly shared the idea that there existed basic principles that should guide human action. In sum, Burke thought the underlying principles of a natural morality and those of political life should match. This idea fed his hostility to the rebels of France.

Burke's assessment of the French Revolution made him a symbol of conservative faith, but it also obscured his repeated efforts in support of reform in his own nation. This perennial symbol of classic conservatism did, indeed, shape his philosophy to allow for the support of specific reforms even if they happened to coincide with particular items of the liberal agenda. In economics he favored the laissez-faire ideas of Adam Smith. As noted, these went by the label "liberal economics" early in the nineteenth century, and at first they were greeted with some skepticism by businessmen who doubted the benefits of competitive free trade unsupported by government. Burke also believed that property was held in trust and ought not to be entirely subjected to the whims of the market. His was a sophisticated and complex conservatism guided by common sense and good judgment. His was a judicious and agile conservatism that brought him fame on both sides of the Atlantic and which the like-minded applauded and invoked for over two centuries.

After Burke, conservative thought in Britain was marked more by its variety than its consistency. A core of Burkean ideas persisted, but thinkers generally thought of as conservatives applied their ideas with significant differences. For example, support for a laissez-faire free-market economy was not shared by all of them, and attitudes toward reform varied. Conservative thinking ranged from a profound fear and even hatred of the democratic movements of the day to an embrace of modest reforms, including a broadening of voting rights, in order to prevent revolutionary upheavals.

A brief and selective list will serve.

Revered poet William Wordsworth greeted the outbreak of the French Revolution with all the hope and optimism of youth. "Bliss was it in that dawn to be alive,/but to be young was very Heaven!" He soon enough lost that glow, turning bitter over the vicious course of events in France. He eventually became an avid Troy: a conservative in politics and sympathetic to the growing troubles of the landed classes in England and to the poor suffering from the abuses of the expanding factory system. Wordsworth returned to religious faith as a devout Anglican and became a committed defender of established tradition. His revolutionary sympathies were long gone when he opposed the Reform Bill of 1832, which only modestly expanded the voting rolls by lowering a bit the property qualification for voting.

Like Wordsworth, his friend and sometime collaborator Samuel Taylor Coleridge embraced a thoroughly conservative view of politics and culture. Both men regretted assaults on religion and saw ruin in the separation of religion from social and political concerns. In defense of the established church and its relation to proper national governance, Coleridge published *On the Constitution of Church and State* in 1829, outlining his religious and political philosophy. Coleridge explicitly rejected the materialist utilitarianism of Jeremy Bentham. He especially worried about the effects of uncontrolled, free-market industrial expansion. Unconvinced that laissez-faire economics would prove self-adjusting, he recognized the need for economic regulation for the common good. Coleridge advocated reforms to ease the suffering of the poor and believed political reforms were necessary to avoid a destabilizing radicalism. His was an activist conservatism aimed at a balance between social stability and progressive change. There was no unyielding affinity for free-enterprise commerce among conservatives of that day.

Another great nineteenth-century voice of conservatism, but one that was also open to change, was that of John Henry Newman. Newman spoke out resolutely against what he considered a dangerous trend in liberal thought concerning religion and church-state relations. An eloquent speaker and masterful writer, he was a major influence on the Church of England, on Catholicism after his conversion, and on the nature of higher education in a changing world. His influence is still felt in these worlds, and his ideas are invoked by authentic conservatives and liberals alike.

Born in London in 1801, Newman was educated at Oxford, became a fellow at Oriel College at the age of 20 and the rector of St. Mary's, Oxford, in 1828. At St. Mary's he soon became famous for his exquisitely crafted sermons delivered to crowds that regularly filled the church to overflowing. Still a young man, he had quickly become a person of note at Oxford and in the Anglican Church, which was about to enter a period of ferment, controversy, and change, in which Newman played no small part. He was increasingly disturbed by what he saw as the spread of liberal religious and political postures at Oxford. He thought the university was following the nation in becoming lax in religious matters.

In 1833 Newman joined the Oxford Movement within the Church of England and soon became its most important voice. The Oxford Movement was ignited in part by developments in British law, which threatened serious changes in the governance of the church. Parliament had recently enacted a series of reforms that enfranchised and opened membership in Parliament to non-Anglicans. In 1828 Protestant dissenters gained political rights long denied them, and electoral restrictions were lifted from Roman Catholics in 1829. What disturbed Newman and others of conservative inclination about these reforms was the odd consequence that Parliament now came to include members who were Protestant dissenters, Roman Catholics, as well as agnostics and an occasional atheist. The Church of England was the nation's established church and the monarch was its head since the days of Henry VIII. Its governance was directly affected by parliamentary legislation, and the new electoral arrangement meant that laws governing the Church of England would now depend on and be influenced by the votes of non-Anglicans and even by the votes of unbelievers. Newman and his friends were especially furious when Parliament, with the votes of such members, passed legislation reorganizing the Anglican dioceses of Ireland.

The Oxford Movement protested that such a church-state relationship was unacceptable. Its members wrote "Tracts for the Times" critical of the new arrangement, and at the same time they mounted a defense of the Church of England as the church most faithful to the apostolic origins of the Christian faith. Newman himself wrote almost a third of the 90 tracts published. He was determined to prove that the Church of England was the *via media* between Protestantism, which had discarded too much of the genuine Christian tradition, and Roman Catholicism, which had added too much that was inauthentic. He threw himself into the study of original sources and the writings of the early Fathers of the church to build his case that the Church of England had best conserved the original faith against the innovations of other Christians. In the course of his studies what he discovered increasingly troubled Newman. Over a period of several years, the evidence, as he read it, drove Newman to the conclusion that it was in fact the Church of England that had altered key elements of the faith that had been preserved by the Roman church. In 1845 he could resist no longer, and to the great distress of many of his Anglican friends, he converted to Roman Catholicism. Newman had joined the Oxford Movement to fight those liberal incursions into church-state relations in Britain and to lead a "high church" conservative Anglicanism against liberal Protestant innovations. His intensive studies, as he explained in his autobiographical *Apologia Pro Vita Sua*, eventually led him to Rome.

His conversion was not without irony. This eloquent and scholarly spokesman for the importance of authentic tradition was regarded with more than a little wariness in Roman Catholic circles and especially in the hierarchy. They suspected Newman of excessive flexibility, especially when he published his most important theological work, *The Development of Doctrine*, shortly after his conversion. In this work he explained that the authentic Christian doctrine of the early church did not change, but, with the passing of generations, doctrines could be understood and expressed differently while remaining true to their original meaning. This was the kind of thinking that had led him to Rome as the depository of the most authentic Christian doctrine. Many in the hierarchy and administration of the Catholic Church missed the nuances of Newman's thought.

Newman was impatient with some of his liberal contemporaries for the implications of their thought, including their rejection of first principles. While he admired Jeremy Bentham's intelligence, he was severely critical of materialism and utilitarianism, and especially of the idea that secular knowledge could in itself lead to moral improvement in individuals and in society. In that regard he was wary of the optimism of both the Enlightenment and the Romantics. Yet Newman was always open to careful distinctions and respectful of opposing views. There is, he once said, "much in the liberalistic theory which is good and true."[10] Conservative in much of his thought, Newman was, nevertheless, an independent thinker of great flexibility and open to modern ideas. He believed that "the Church's creed had grown by a sure and gradual process, assimilating elements from all sides, and changing as the centuries passed."[11] He supported a larger role for the laity in the church, an idea in advance of the age. He had no problem with Darwin and the idea of evolution as did many, especially in evangelical Protestant circles. He thought the ultra-conservative "Syllabus of Errors" (see below) issued by Pope Pius IX was an embarrassment. He also argued against the first Vatican Council defining papal infallibility; he fully respected the authority of the pope, but he thought such a proclamation was inopportune. He applauded the new critical biblical and theological scholarship of his day, which disturbed the more timid and fearful. This broad-minded Newman was regarded as somewhat dangerous and treated with suspicion for much of this life in the Catholic Church. The veil of suspicion was not lifted until Pope Leo XIII made Newman a cardinal at the age of 90. Advanced age renders subversives less fearsome, but in this case a wise Leo also recognized Newman's genius and his gift to the church.

Here then was a leading conservative voice of the nineteenth century who personified intellectual rigor and was open to the change to which it led. He argued repeatedly that reasoned change must be welcomed. That idea came through clearly in what is probably his most widely known work, *The Idea of a University*. Here Newman presents the enduring argument for higher education in the liberal arts as the best vehicle for the development of a sophisticated mind, versed in tradition and open to the challenges of an ever-changing world. It is a book of which so much of the contemporary American university community is shamefully ignorant. Newman insists that the aim of a liberal university education is not the inculcation of virtue. That function lies elsewhere as does narrow vocational training. The function of an undergraduate liberal education is not to produce a "Christian, not the Catholic, but the gentleman. It is well to be a gentleman, it is well to have a cultivate intellect, a delicate taste, a candid, equitable dispassionate mind, a noble courteous bearing in the conduct of life." These should be the objects of a liberal education, but they are "no guarantee of sanctity or even conscientiousness"; "its object is nothing more or less than intellectual excellence."[12]

Newman stands as a model of a nineteenth-century intellectual who cherished and broadcast conservative values while insisting on openness to challenges of the modern world. Newman was a conservative who, in some ways, sparked a revolution. His ideas came alive in the twentieth century when he became a major inspiration for the great wave of changes that came to Catholicism during the Second Vatican Council. Newman's life and thought stand as evidence that many traditional conservatives were not stodgy nay-sayers opposed to every suggestion of change, but imaginative thinkers who could defend tradition while adapting to the march of time. But there is no hint in Newman's thought that the unfettered individual pursuing self-interest should constitute some kind of conservative ideal.

There were other voices who exemplified nineteenth-century British conservative thought ranging from the stiffly rigid to sensibly flexible.

Historian and politician Thomas Babington Macaulay saw the British Reform Act of 1832 as a step in the direction of universal suffrage and a great mistake. Broad suffrage, he believed, was incompatible with all forms of government and invited revolution.

Philosopher, essayist, and historian Thomas Carlyle wrote a three-volume account of the French Revolution in 1837 and, like Burke, passionately condemned the violence and destabilizing actions of the rebels. Carlyle had no sympathy for democracy, which he believed to be a foolish idea, disastrous morally as well as politically. Accordingly he was hostile to electoral reform and another expansion of voting rights in the proposed Reform Bill of 1867. The masses were not capable of governing, but neither was the hereditary elite. Government should be the activity of the ablest in society; how such were to be selected and empowered he did not clearly address. Carlyle's conservatism also harbored a profound dislike for the new market economy of the age and saw capitalism, too, in need of restraint.

Benjamin Disraeli combined with some success openness to change and reform with a commitment to a fundamentally conservative posture toward tradition, stable government, and a culture of higher values. Unlike the extreme, antidemocratic wing of his Tory Party, Disraeli sympathized with the plight of the working class in the face of the ruthless power and abuses of the industrial and merchant class. His more moderate Tory following was somewhat paternalistic toward labor and hostile to the growing free-trade sentiment in Britain. The Liberal Party of Gladstone was more welcoming of laissez-faire economics and opposed to strong government intervention in business matters. Disraeli strongly supported the Reform Act of 1867, which extended voting rights to many more men including some urban workers. This offended his more fervently conservative Tory colleagues, but Disraeli believed these new voters could be won over to support the traditions of the monarchy and the church. During his term as prime minister from 1874 to 1880, he led a reformist government that passed an array of laws including provisions for public health services, a program to build working-class housing, support for public education, and factory laws to improve working conditions and worker rights. As a kind of Tory democrat, he was convinced of the need to lessen the vast economic gap between the rich and the working class. All this he saw as a *conservative* program in line with the work he did to preserve and strengthen the monarchy and defend it against growing criticism. He often spoke in defense of the peerage, the union of church and state, and other traditional elements of the British constitution.

Winston Churchill pursued a similar strategy in the next century cooperating in reform efforts for conservative purposes. Defenders have argued that Disraeli and Churchill were conservatives who saw social reform as a way to make industrialism and capitalism compatible with tradition and conservative values. This is a lesson apparently unlearned among twenty-first-century politicians who pose as conservatives.

It seems clear that conservatism in nineteenth-century Britain was not a simple handmaid in the service of capital, but a complex and somewhat varied collection of ideas. There was a shared base of reverence for tradition, religion, and stable culture, with a variety of positions on the role of the masses and on the appropriate response of government toward the growing power and influence of industrial and merchant capitalism. Liberals were more fervently committed to free-market ideas, but on a number of issues it was difficult to delineate clear differences between conservatives and liberals of the day. Reform measures culminating in the great Reform Act of 1832 in Britain were the exception in the early nineteenth-century Europe, and perhaps helped Britain escape the explosion of uprisings that burst across the continent in 1848. The picture was different elsewhere in Europe, where the emerging character of conservative thought was more doctrinaire and less malleable than that in Britain.

~~~

On the Continent, the French Revolution and the Napoleonic era that followed produced a traumatic response from established authorities in Europe that was neither surprising nor entirely unreasonable. Robespierre and the Terror worked assiduously to destroy all remnants of the Old Regime including monarchy, aristocracy, and the Catholic Church in France. After the fall of Robespierre and the Jacobins, the ruling Directory, a weak dictatorship by a committee of five, took control of France. They assured the profiteers from the sale of confiscated church properties that there would be no return to monarchy and their gains were safe. These assurances could not make up for inept governance and widespread popular discontent. When that discontent bred riots and a resurgence of die-hard royalists in October 1795, the Directory called on an artillery officer named Napoleon Bonaparte to clear the streets. This he did with a famous "whiff of grapeshot." Rewarded with important military commands, Napoleon soon became a national hero. Recognizing an almost universal disgust toward a brutal and corrupt government, Napoleon seized power in 1799 in a coup d'état that overthrew the Directory.

With a keen sense of the psychological needs of a people exhausted by foreign war and domestic chaos, he announced that the Revolution was over. After 10 years of disorder, fear, and bloodshed, this was a welcome message. Napoleon brought some iron-fisted stability to France, but he also imposed draconian restrictions on civil liberties, continued an expansionist campaign of endless warfare, and converted the first French Republic into a Napoleonic empire. (The French are now enjoying life under the Fifth Republic. After a restored monarchy, two empires, and five republics, the French will undoubtedly keep trying until they get it right.) Napoleon made Pope Pius VII a virtual prisoner and forced him to sign the Concordat of 1801, conceding to a religious settlement in France on Napoleon's terms. With his gift for dramatic spectacle, Napoleon staged his own coronation as emperor as a reprise of the papal coronation of Charlemagne. But in the modern replay, the pope was made to serve merely as an altar prop. For all the world to see in Jacques David's commemorative painting of the coronation ceremony, Napoleon crowned himself. The Revolution had threatened the very existence of monarchy everywhere, and Napoleon's despotic reign added 15 more years of upheaval to the life of France and all of Europe. After the humiliating retreat from a disastrous Russian campaign in 1812 and a crushing defeat of the French at the hands of the united armies of Britain, Prussia, Russia, and Austria in 1814, the rather generous victors allowed Napoleon to live comfortably in exile in the lovely island of Elba. They misunderstood his unquenchable ambition. The Congress of Vienna was sent into panic with the news of Napoleon's escape, and it took more fighting and a final defeat at the hands of the Duke of Wellington to end the Napoleonic era. There would be no escape from his new place of exile at St. Helena in the south Atlantic, 4,500 miles from Paris. After so many years of turmoil it is no surprise that conservatives were driven to react and retrench.

After Napoleon's final demise at Waterloo, the Congress of Vienna organized the Quadruple Alliance dedicated to united intervention to prevent new revolutions. The chief architect of the program, Prince Klemens von Metternich, interpreted any move toward reform as a prelude to revolution. His influence imposed an era of repression across Europe for decades. Rulers of the major powers lived in constant fear of renewed revolutionary activity. The restored Bourbon kings of France, Louis XVIII and Charles X; Tsar Nicholas of Russia; and Austria's Metternich united in their resistance to change. They rejected any suggestion of reform, repressed student and worker associations, and were quick to label as radical the merely suspicious. In an essay entitled "A Political Confession of Faith" in 1820, Metternich warned his contemporaries: "Two elements alone remain in all their strength, and never cease to exercise their indestructible influence with equal power. These are the precepts of morality, religious as well as social, and the necessities created by locality. From the time that men attempt to swerve from these bases to become rebels against these sovereign arbiters of their destinies, society suffers from a malaise which sooner or later will lead to a state of convulsion." He called on governments to be strong, just, beneficent, but watchful and strict.

Britain did not entirely escape the mood of the post-Vienna world. The government responded to protests against worsening economic conditions for the working class with force, the suspension of *habeas corpus*, and police spies. In August 1819, mounted troops charged into a peaceful demonstration in support of economic and political reform at St. Peter's Field in Manchester. Poet Percy Shelly marked the moment in his poem "England in 1819" in which one line refers to "A people starved and stabbed in th' untilled field." The dead and wounded that day numbered dozens, and the event was sarcastically dubbed the "Peterloo Massacre." A shaken Parliament responded to these early rumblings for reform with the passage of a spate of laws called the Six Acts that severely restricted British civil liberties. In a few years the repressive mood in Britain softened, and between 1828 and 1834 Parliament passed a series of reforms that eased tensions and perhaps avoided more serious violence.

Across the Channel there was no such release of pressure. The ruling regimes of Europe took Metternich's warnings seriously and installed programs of repression everywhere. Spain closely imitated Metternich's policies as did the smaller states in Germany and Italy. Russia was the most repressive country in Europe. This conservative panic about the possibility of renewed revolution and the repression of reform movements eventually proved ineffective against a tide of change. The French Revolution had failed with a mix of tragedy, irony, and farce. As those statues of Voltaire and Rousseau were raised and honored, the streets of Paris ran red with the blood of guillotined thousands, most of whom, it is seldom noted in textbooks, were not aristocrats or clergy, but workers and peasants. (In 1989 there were debates in Paris about whether the 200th anniversary of the Revolution should be an occasion of celebration or mourning.) But while the French Revolution spiraled out of control and into the hands of extremists of vicious character, the ideals it broadcast and the American success in implementing those ideals continued to influence and inspire. Metternich and his allies could not eliminate calls for reform, and Europe experienced growing tension and pressure until the explosions of 1848.

Across Europe middle class liberal reformers agitated for economic and electoral changes. Metternich labeled them fakes who claimed to speak for "the people," when their real objective was to replace the aristocracy as the ruling class. He had a point. The bourgeoisie led many of the reform efforts in a quest for greater political influence, and they succeeded in recruiting workers and peasants to their cause. But working-class interests and objectives differed significantly from those of the middle class, and the American example of extending the franchise to the un-propertied encouraged working-class demands for entry into the political process in Europe. The middle class wanted access to the halls of government, but they were not entirely sanguine about opening the doors wide enough for entry by the masses. Conflicting ambitions boded trouble for European reform.

Those troubles came later. Immediately after 1815 the problem for reformers was the program of repression launched by governments across Europe. The restored Bourbon monarchy in France feared any concessions to reform. The new regime borrowed from Napoleon's example and used secret police and provocateurs to unmask reformers and radicals alike. Repressive policies, especially under Charles X, stalled but could not eliminate reform activity. The middle and working class united in what was a comparatively moderate revolution in 1830. With little bloodshed, the rising displaced Charles and brought Louis-Philippe, the Duke of Orleans, to the throne with a promise of republican reforms. The right to vote was, indeed, expanded, but to less than 4 percent of French men. The revolt of 1830 proved a small victory for the bourgeois industrial and merchant class, and offered little to workers or peasants, and a new wave of repression by the government of Louis-Philippe followed his broken promises of reform. The thirst for change among reform and radical groups went unquenched.

The pattern was similar elsewhere. A liberal middle class agitated for more democratic practice; they enlisted workers to support the cause, but this proved to be an uneasy alliance. Stubborn reactionary regimes hounded reformers and radicals with equal determination and brutality. Beneath what seemed to be a controlled surface, pressure continued to build. Alexis De Tocqueville, whose keen eye had produced the insightful analysis of American society, *Democracy in America*, now assessed the situation at home and thought that Europe was ready to explode. Beginning in 1845, a series of poor harvest raised the price of bread beyond the reach of the poor and lit the fuse of Europe's powder keg.

The explosion came early in 1848 with the outbreak of spontaneous, uncoordinated revolts across the continent. Over 50 revolutions, large and small, shocked the ruling classes. Despite years of worry and well-oiled machines of repression, rebel victories came with surprising speed and ease. Old regimes collapsed after only a few weeks of turmoil and relatively little bloodshed. Louis-Philippe, no doubt aware of revolutionary treatment of royalty in France, prudently fled to exile in England. Metternich resigned his post after decades of dominance in Austria. The victorious coalitions of workers, peasants, and middle class rebels celebrated their easy victory and prepared to govern. The joy was short lived, and the hard task of governing destroyed the fragile alliance. Middle class leaders had recruited workers to man the barricades. Now those workers were bold enough to demand a share of power. The bourgeoisie had wanted to break the aristocratic grip on power with more democratic government, but the idea of extending the power to vote and hold office to the mass of workers and peasants was not a congenial thought. Workers chanted demands for social and economic changes that would have to be paid for by higher wages and new taxes. Those wages and taxes would have to be paid by the propertied and the business classes. Conservative disdain for the masses found new appeal among the liberal leaders of the revolutions who called on the military to quell worker agitation and preserve good order. This they did with unrestrained violence. By the summer liberal provisional governments collapsed or produced newly conservative constitutions. Genuine democratic reforms survived almost nowhere; Piedmont-Sardinia under Victor Emanuel was one of the few exceptions.

After some months the Second Republic in France foundered, and the French brought the nephew of Napoleon to power. He soon dissolved the second try at republican government in order to establish the Second Empire. This invention he ruled with a make-believe elected legislature that had no significant power. In Prussia the leadership of the revolution fell to a group of intellectuals, university professors, and students where, it is said, they talked the new government to death. One need not harbor deeply conservative prejudices to eschew any revolution led by university professors. Soon Otto von Bismarck governed an autocratic Prussia and went about building a united and militaristic Germany hungry for arms and empire. Workers across Europe, with good reason to feel betrayed by their liberal middle class allies, migrated toward socialist and other radical groups. Only days before the revolutions of 1848 broke out, Karl Marx and Frederick Engels published their *Communist Manifesto* that ended with the stirring appeal, "Workers of the world unite. You have nothing to lose but your chains." Many heard the call.

Conservative fears were realized; their fears seemed justified, but their response was flawed. Rather than applying a reasoned conservatism, the response of the ruling classes of Europe was rigid and reactionary. They tended to read modern developments as threats to the survival of civilization itself. Burke's warnings about events in France seemed prophetic, and others joined in shaping a conservative ideology, but even as it constructed that ideology, a conservative Europe failed to respond effectively to the demands for change that had been unleashed by the French Revolution and by the continuing success of the American experiment.

~~~

The French Revolution, Napoleon's dictatorship, and the events that followed inspired the development of conservative thought on the continent. As Burke attacked the French Revolution from his British perspective, Joseph de Maistre was its best known and most virulent critic on the continent. His revulsion over events in France was rooted in an extreme and uncompromising conservative mindset. De Maistre knew and applauded Burke's analysis of the Revolution in France, and he shared much of Burke's conservative outlook. He was, however, more overtly religious in his prescriptions. He was deeply moved by *Reflections*, whose French edition he read in 1791. He acknowledged a debt to Burke and shared a disdain for the leaders of the Revolution. He especially appreciated Burke's condemnation of Rousseau, who, he too believed, inspired the revolt. With the iron confidence that sometimes infects the intensely religious, he claimed to know God's will and saw God's punishing hand in human calamities. He attacked the vulgarity of mass society, and he was more inclined than Burke to emphasize order over liberty.

De Maistre was born in Savoy, then part of the Kingdom of Piedmont-Sardinia, where his family of French origin had moved decades earlier. He fled Savoy into exile in Italy in 1792 ahead of an invading French revolutionary army. In later years he served his king as minister to Russia for almost 15 years, until 1817. During his exile and diplomatic service, he wrote voluminously on the Revolution and its consequences. His work won high praise for its style, sharp arguments, his keen eye for the weaknesses of rationalist thought, and the excessively optimistic ideas of Enlightenment thinkers. His power as a writer made him widely read and broadly influential on nineteenth-century conservative thought. Hitting a chord that resonated through conservative thinking, de Maistre dismissively rejected the idea that human evil can be eliminated or mitigated by education or an improved social and economic environment. In the eighteenth century Enlightenment thinkers circulated such meliorist ideas with enthusiastic faith, and the thought survived strongly among social reformers in the nineteenth century. But de Maistre saw man as a sinful creature: weak, proud, and in constant need of control and direction by strong authority both political and religious. Like Burke, he condemned the French philosophes of the Enlightenment as intellectuals who not only undermined the old regime but also eroded the stability of society itself. It is a notable irony that among the philosophers who had encouraged a sharp break with traditional institutions, more than a few of them were compelled to flee from the perils of the Terror.

De Maistre's views on politics in France had not begun in bitterness. He once thought reforms necessary and applauded those who pressured Louis XVI into calling together the Estates General in 1789, the action that in fact began the Revolution. His views quickly changed in August, when the National Assembly abandoned feudal titles and privileges and issued the *Declaration of the Rights of Man*, providing, at least theoretically, an equality of citizenship. Like Burke he was outraged at the confiscation of church property, and he read the Revolution as disastrously radical even before its first year had ended and two years *before* the Terror began. In 1796 he published *Considerations on France*, in which he pronounced that the Terror was divine punishment visited on France. He recalled the old order as idyllic in contrast to the pain and chaos unleashed by the Revolution. In the years that followed, his writing insisted that legitimate government required a religious foundation, and he looked to the restoration of authoritative Christian monarchies ruling Europe and an assertive papacy leading the way as it had in the Middle Ages. This outlook was, perhaps, a product of the trauma of the Revolution inspiring an excessively sentimental reading of history. The modern world had little to offer de Maistre. He lacked the flexibility of Burke, and while much of his thought embraced the fundamental creed of conservatives of his day, his political posture might be more appropriately described as reactionary rather than conservative.

Less well known than de Maistre but also influential was Louis Vicomte de Bonald, a leading counterrevolutionary writer and another voice influenced by Burke's writing. He too was an émigré who fled France early in the Revolution. He returned later, bitter at what the rebels had wrought and no less hostile to Napoleonic rule. He became politically active after the Bourbon restoration and served in the government of Louis XVIII. In that service he chaired a censorship commission and clamped down on the press. Bonald wrote a defense of a religiously rooted absolute monarchy. Society and law came from God and required religious guidance. Church and state should be united, and, reviving a medieval idea, he insisted that monarchs acted in the name of God. These elements were essential to a stable society, and he believed the forces unleashed by the Revolution threatened the very survival of Western civilization.

In the nineteenth century, the papacy was another barricade of resistance to liberal ideas. In mid-century Pope Pius IX began his pontificate as somewhat more liberal than his immediate predecessors and was open to reform ideas even in the governance of the Papal States over which he ruled. Liberal-leaning Catholics were encouraged, hoping the new pope would smile on their proposals for reform. Then the revolutions of 1848 changed his worldview. His secretary of state was assassinated, and Pius himself had to flee from the Vatican in disguise. It is remarkable but not surprising how quickly conservative ideas impress themselves when radicals threaten assassination. His ideological conversion was quick, complete, and intense. In 1864 he attached his famous "Syllabus of Errors" to an encyclical warning against liberal ideas. The list condemned atheism and materialism, as one might expect from a pontiff, but it also went on to reject a long list of liberal ideas including separation of church and state and freedom of religion. To cover any points that might have been overlooked, the last "error" listed was the proposition that "The Roman Pontiff can, and ought to reconcile himself and come to terms with progress, liberalism, and modern civilization." Those outside the church scoffed, and many Catholics, including the celebrated convert and hardly radical John Henry Newman, blushed.

Even as the influence of the papacy receded in world affairs, the perceived assaults on the church by modernity moved Pius IX to reassert papal authority. He called together the first Vatican Council for the approval of a statement of papal infallibility. The pope had already lost the Papal States to the Italian unification movement, and repeated assertions of papal authority could not prevent Italian forces from taking Rome itself in 1870. The conservative outlook of Pius IX insisted that an effective papacy required the possession of temporal power. In his fury at the loss of his territories, Pius vowed never to leave the grounds of the Vatican. His precedent was followed by each successor until an agreement with the Italian government in 1929, when the papacy abandoned its territorial claims and confined itself to the control only of Vatican City. History proved Pius wrong in his judgment about temporal power. Removal from the burdens and liabilities of civil government freed the papacy and the church from contentious and sometimes ugly political controversy, and both the church and the papacy benefited as a result.

The hierarchy of the Catholic Church never completely recovered from the attacks and trauma generated by the French Revolution and Napoleon, and the political tensions precipitated by the outbreaks in 1848. Pius IX felt besieged in a hostile world that was losing its faith, and he lashed out at it with little discrimination among the elements of modernity. Through his sweeping condemnation of the reforming impulses of the times, the pope allied his church with a reactionary system of monarchy and aristocracy in a Europe where both were decaying, dying, or dead. The alienation of many of the progressive and working-class faithful was one sad result. Whatever their religious convictions, many nineteenth-century conservatives, especially in Europe, shared the pope's distrust of modern developments and classed them as destabilizing and dangerous. Those fears often blocked the ability to distinguish between the dangerous, the benign, and the beneficent in modern thought.

Less hostile to modern developments was Alexis de Tocqueville. He toured the United States in the 1830s and wrote the classic analysis of American society. He served briefly in the regime of Louis-Philippe and helped in preparing a new constitution during the revolution of 1848. Because he supported measures to establish order and resist extremists, he is sometimes described as a conservative. Some ideas he did hold in common with conservative thinkers. For example, in his critique of American democracy he worried about leveling to the lowest common denominator, a cheapening of culture, and the possibility of the tyranny of the majority. Nevertheless, read in its entirety, his analysis of the United States celebrated the American democratic experiment despite its unconservative implications. At home in France he urged reforms, supported the idea of a broadened suffrage, and recommended constitutional structures similar to those in America. If, indeed, he is to be classed as a conservative, he was among those who saw the necessity for change in order to preserve and strengthen stability and established values.

One is struck by the variety of opinion and specific points of dissent among European conservatives, as among the British, but there were elements in common that united their thought. Focus on the French Revolution as a great disaster was everywhere unanimous among conservatives. That trauma was difficult for conservatives to overcome and soured many on the very idea of reform. Reforms, it was thought by the most fervent conservatives, were inherently mischievous, would never satisfy the reformers, and would inevitably lead to a repeat of revolutionary disaster. Conservatives in common condemned the misuse of reason by the philosophes of the Enlightenment and held them responsible for disparaging tradition and inciting revolt. They were often critical of the growing emphasis on individual rights and the decline of concern for the community, which protected and empowered individuals. They distrusted the working class and were little inclined to extend political rights in that direction. There was, even among the less faithfully observant, a deep concern over the decline of respect for religion, which they deemed essential for social stability. Commercial and material utility they blamed for a coarsening of the culture. Conservatives who were not themselves deeply involved in commercial or industrial enterprise were troubled by the growing influence of business interests, and even in the early stage of the Industrial Revolution, they saw a need for government supervision. Conservatives did not deem the support of capitalism as an economic system to be a necessary adjunct of conservative ideology. Laissez-faire economics and the uncritical encouragement of industrial and commercial enterprise were more clearly part of the liberal agenda for much of the nineteenth century. This would change before the century ended.

2

Conservative and Liberal
in Early America

Conservatives in America shared some of the concerns of their
European brothers, but the ideology took on a somewhat different
complexion across the Atlantic. From the start, life in the new nation
was much freer, more democratic, and quicker to entertain change.
After all the Americans were revolutionaries, a label not lightly
employed by conservatives. Not only did they join the revolt for
independence, but they also subscribed to the idea of human equality
and democratic government, ideas rejected by European conservatives, and even by most of the otherwise innovative and antitraditional
thinkers of the Enlightenment. There was not a genuine democrat
among them. Even John Locke reserved parliamentary supremacy to
the control of a very small, elite electorate. Enlightenment philosophes
wanted governments to run on rational principles, and broad participation in government did not seem reasonable to them. They had no
experience with democracy; they did not see it as a rationally defen-
sible form of government, and they thought the Americans odd and
quixotic. What the British and Europeans generally did not understand was that Americans had for many decades developed institutions of local, albeit colonial, government chosen by broad electorates
and already exercising a large measure of independence from British
control. Every colony had its own elected assembly, and in an agrarian
society land ownership was common enough to generate broad suffrage. It has been argued that the Americans fought a revolution not
to establish democracy, but to defend and preserve self-governing
democracies that already existed. In Europe the sophisticated conservatives were first amused; then they scoffed, and then they worried
about the example this experiment would set for their own people.

In America the political divisions that formed during and after the
revolution were not about the establishment of republican government, but about the character and control of that government.
While the colonies were willing enough to unite against Britain, each

was jealous of its own independence, and, having just rebelled against one strong central authority, they were reluctant to submit to the rule of another. So the new government of the United States established under the Articles of Confederation was a weak one that required agreement among 9 of the 13 states for action and unanimity for really important action. The makers of the new country cherished their independence and their commitment to republicanism. The liberal among them hoped to make democratic participation as wide as possible in a broadly egalitarian society. The more conservative founders shared the republican commitment, but they also thought property holding and the means to protect it were essential to a stable society. The challenge to the new nation was to blend and adjust those contrasting views of government while holding the union together. The genius and great gift of the early American experience was precisely that ability to bring enough compromise to liberal and conservative issues to sustain an effective and enduring union.

The United States under the Articles of Confederation suffered a measure of social and political turmoil with more than a suggestion of class conflict. Shays' Rebellion in Massachusetts, a protest of yeoman farmers against unforgiving mortgage foreclosures, gave some of the most enthusiastic supporters of the American Revolution pause. In 1786 Daniel Shays organized an armed band of Berkshire Valley farmers, some of them veterans of the revolution, demanding tax relief and a moratorium on debts. Marching from town to town, they did with some success for a time block courts from authorizing the confiscation and sale of farm properties. Those of conservative outlook were not alone in worry. It was clear the Americans were engaged in an experiment, the outcome of which was not comfortably clear. Shays' foray, economic uncertainties, and political unrest under the Articles convinced many that a more stable government capable of sustaining foreign credit and domestic order required a new constitutional structure. The view was hardly unanimous, and the struggle for ratification of the new Constitution of 1787 was hard fought and proved a close call in a number of states. Rhode Island even refused to join the new government until after Washington was inaugurated and the new government was underway.

Once the Constitution was ratified, however, both those who argued the need for stronger government and those who feared it blessed the new pact. The arguments thereafter centered on how to *interpret* the document. Did the Constitution confer a narrow grant of power, implicitly forbidding what it did not explicitly grant, or was it a broad concession of power blocking only what was expressly forbidden to the government? While the labels lack precision, it is notable that from that first great American political battle the federalists, who looked for a strong, agile, and authoritative central government, are generally remembered as the conservatives who formed the Federalist Party. The anti-federalist movement that evolved into Thomas Jefferson's Democratic Republican political party planted the seeds of the American liberal tradition. The application of the labels "conservative" and "liberal" will later change as attitudes toward government changed, and understanding that shift requires context.

The organizers of the Federalist Party, especially strong in New England, had played an important role in the revolution, in drafting a new constitution, and in serving the Washington administration. Besides anxiety from the fresh memory of Shays' Rebellion, conservatives also fretted over a brief outburst of violence in western Pennsylvania in 1794. Troops sent by President Washington quelled the "Whiskey Rebellion," which protested a tax on the profitable conversion of corn into more easily transported liquor. That episode reinforced the conservative commitment to a strong and effective federal government as they worried about the consequences of too much democracy. In line with their European counterparts, theirs was not an optimistic view of human nature. Men's passions required control, and a stable society needed a government strong enough to maintain order. Federalists were generally appalled by the revolutionary events in France and feared the excesses could be imitated in America. Many were involved in commerce and saw an important role for the government to support business enterprise for the sake of national prosperity, and, not incidentally, their own. Toward this end they supported closer relations with Britain, the dominant trading partner of the United States despite the revolution.

Much of this Federalist agenda clashed with the anti-Federalists who looked to Thomas Jefferson to lead the opposition. Jefferson was a child of the Enlightenment, but his commitment to Enlightenment rationalism was infused with a strong element of Romanticism. His Romantic vision focused on a reverence for nature, his hopes for an agrarian society, a faith in the common man, his egalitarianism, and his deeply embedded commitment to democracy. As the principal author of the Declaration of Independence, Jefferson wrote for the ages. This slave owner knew that slavery was an aberration, and he did not limit or qualify his proclamation of human equality. He also had a deep faith in the ability of ordinary men to govern prudently. Human life, liberty, and equality Jefferson posited as self-evident. As children of the Creator all people own a fundamental human dignity, which differences of ancestry or wealth cannot erase. They are not granted by a government with power to alter them. These rights are inalienable because they are inherent and permanent, conferred by the Creator. That is why all, and especially governments, are obliged to protect these rights. According to Jefferson's dictum, in the face of extreme threats to these rights by a government, revolution is not only permitted; it is required. These were radical ideas for their time, but Americans, conservative and liberal, harnessed them for their new experiment.

An agrarian in a still overwhelmingly agrarian country, Jefferson believed the yeoman farmer would work fervently to defend his freedom and would serve as the backbone of democracy. Jefferson invested great hope—too much for too long—in the idea that the French Revolution would produce positive political and social advances. He hoped the French adventure would spark a genuine movement for freedom and democracy across Europe. His experience during years of diplomatic service in Europe convinced him that strong central governments were inevitably oppressive and that the new industrialism, however fruitful for a few, bred poverty and suffering for the working masses. These ideas governed much of Jefferson's political thinking before and during his presidency.

Jefferson was the American minister to France while the new constitution was being written in Philadelphia in 1787. He worried the convention was crafting the charter for a new more powerful central government, and his friend and ally James Madison had to convince him to embrace the new constitution. This he did by reading the document as a very narrow grant of powers to the government. For Jefferson, if a particular power of the national government was not specified, one should assume it did not exist. A practical man as well as an ideologue, he suspended this principle during his own presidency, when he proposed that the treaty making power *implied* the ability of the government to purchase new lands. This was a powerful implication by which Jefferson doubled the size of the nation through the Louisiana Purchase from Napoleon at a bargain price. On other issues in his competition with Alexander Hamilton, Jefferson proved more consistent in defending severe limits to federal power. He opposed Hamilton's proposal for a federally chartered national bank, and he had to be dragged into a compromise on the accumulation of a national debt. In this competition, President Washington more often sided with Hamilton and the Federalist viewpoint. Jefferson fiercely opposed and campaigned against the repressive Alien and Sedition Acts passed during the administration of John Adams. In protest he joined with Madison in writing the Virginia and Kentucky Resolutions to defend states' rights against this federal intrusion and insisted on a strict constructionist reading of the constitution. So in those early days of the Republic, the most liberal figure in American politics opposed a strong federal government and supported states' rights as the best defense of individual freedom. By the end of the nineteenth century the American nation grew and changed in ways that led liberals to abandon these ideas and convinced conservatives to adopt them.

Alexander Hamilton is often listed among the early American conservative gods, but he was hardly a respecter of tradition. He conceived and engineered policies to encourage the development of an industrial America, unleashing some very unconservative trends. As President Washington's secretary of the treasury, Hamilton championed an economic program including proposals for a national bank, the federal assumption of state debts to establish the nation's credit, federal trade regulations, and an effective tax system. He was confident these policies would stimulate economic expansion. Hamilton forecast the future intimacy between capitalist enterprise and conservative politics, though conservatives of his age did not shrink from supporting a strong and effective national government. Historians and biographers argue whether Hamilton was a genuine conservative or simply an opportunist of the right. He was certainly an elitist, deeply suspicious of the mass of men and firm in the faith that the well-to-do should govern. Society was better represented, he thought, by a natural aristocracy, and for him wealth was a reliable marker of natural talent. The propertied, after all, had more to lose and would more likely govern carefully and prudently. His concern was for good order, and good order was always at risk given the faults of human nature. He wanted a government strong enough to stimulate and regulate the national economy and tried to mix a measure of mercantilist control with free enterprise. He was a strong defender of the rights and privileges of property as well as the taxing power of the new government, and he despised the revolutionary French and all they stood for. At the constitutional convention Hamilton argued for lifetime terms for the Senate, and even hoped for a monarch-like president for life. He once remarked that "it will probably be found expedient to go into the British form." Evidence of his embrace of tradition and conservative ethical, social, and religious values is less clear. One historian describes him as a conservative with so many qualifications that "he was the only one of his kind."[1]

There is less disagreement about the conservative credentials of John Adams, whom Russell Kirk calls the founder of true conservatism in America. His posture was clear and consistent in support of individual liberty *and* effective government, which he believed necessary both to restrain and to protect the people. In John Adams, one can recognize important differences between European and American conservatism. He was, after all, a revolutionary and among the most insistent advocates of independence. He embraced republican ideals and the conviction that ordinary people could responsibly share in governance with a faith and hope that his fellow conservatives in Europe could not share. Adams was a farmer in a nation of yeoman farmers. Such toilers were called peasants in the Old World, and the idea that peasants, seldom literate in eighteenth-century Europe, should vote and hold office was a challenge to reason. Adams's American experience taught him differently, and the democratic faith that had impelled his revolutionary fervor remained with him. But once independence was won, the conservative instincts in Adams came to the surface.

With some reservations his was a Burkean conservatism. A New Englander of long ancestry, he greatly respected tradition and order. He believed religion and the values it sustained were vital to a healthy society. Adams thought men capable of virtue, but his was a sober view of human nature. He believed men equal in rights, under the law and under God, but he rejected the Enlightenment notion that men were perfectible by education or environment. He called this idea of human perfectibility "mischievous nonsense."[2] Rather he saw human action moved by passion, greed, and lust for power. Men could govern themselves, but ought to be led by the natural aristocracy that dwelt among them with suffrage limited by sufficient property holdings, and he hoped these would be broadly enjoyed. He was acutely sensitive to the potential abuse of power and to its easy corruption, even when exercised by natural elites. So he argued for a division and balance of power among the branches of government even as he supported the idea of a strong executive. The function of government was to promote virtue and limit the effects of passion in the people. His was a realist's conservatism.

When Adams served in the American delegation to Paris with Benjamin Franklin during the American Revolution, he came to despise the European philosophes and the disciples of Rousseau, as did Burke. He saw mischief in their ideas about man and society. When the French Revolution began, Adams applauded the declaration of reforming ideas broadcast by the rebels, but he soon concluded that developments in Paris would deteriorate into chaos and tyranny. He soured on the French Revolution much more quickly than his friend Jefferson. He feared the Revolution could let loose anarchy in the world and undermine both government and religion with disastrous consequences for a society of good order. While he shared much of Burke's political philosophy and Burke's revulsion against the horror that the rebels brought to France, Adams's conservatism could not embrace Burke's admiration for monarchy and hereditary aristocracy. Adams marked a clear and distinct difference between American and European conservatives. In his diary he wrote, "Government is nothing more than the combined force of society, or the united power of the multitude for the peace, order, safety, good and happiness of the people. . . . There is no king or queen bee distinguished from all others . . . in the human hive. No man has yet produced any revelation from heaven in his favor, any divine communication to govern his fellow men. Nature throws us all into the world equal and alike." Echoing a consistently conservative view of his age, he wrote, "The preservation of liberty depends upon the intellectual and moral character of the people. As long as knowledge and virtue are diffused generally among the body of a nation, it is impossible they should be enslaved." Adams combined his commitment to democracy with a conservative reading of what was necessary to make democracy successful. He recognized "that the multitudes are convinced that the people should have a voice, a share, and be made an integral part; and that the government should be a mixture, and such a combination of the powers of one, the few and the many, as is best calculated to check and control each other, and oblige all to cooperate in this one democratic principle, that the end of all government is the happiness of the people." This was his understanding of the American experiment, which he urged on European governments. With some prescience, even before the outbreak of revolution in France, he believed there should be some accommodation with democratic desires in Europe lest they risk "total revolution in religion and government."[3]

The American conservative commitment to both liberty and order posed a problem for Adams when he became president. During his administration troubles with revolutionary France and fear of excessive French influence in the United States launched the first outburst of xenophobia in America. A Federalist-dominated Congress passed the Alien and Sedition Acts, a set of laws that made it more difficult for newcomers to become citizens and also empowered the government to prosecute persons who criticized the federal government. The targets of prosecution included newspaper editors, and those prosecuted turned out to be supporters of Jefferson. Adams had signed the laws and became associated with repression, an impression that contributed heavily to his defeat in the election of 1800. Like other experiments, the American democratic adventure involved some trial and error.

John Quincy Adams, deeply devoted to his father, carried on the family tradition of commitment to conservative ideals, but with certain deviations and adjustments. He struck a unique political posture that makes it difficult to categorize him as a pure conservative. He broke away from the Federalist Party of his father and joined Jefferson's Democratic-Republicans. But he came to reject their states' rights narrowness in favor of his vision of a federal government whose obligation it was to promote the material, intellectual, and moral improvement of society. The younger Adams shared the conservative prejudice that government should be the business of the best, ablest, and most virtuous of men, but he also clung to the more liberal belief that human progress and improvement was part of a providential plan. He, too, wanted a government strong enough to command international respect and promote domestic good order and civic virtue based on solid moral principles. His fundamental conservatism was also colored somewhat by an openness to change. As president he wanted to expand the government's role to actively participate in national growth and development. His message to Congress in November 1825 called for the passage of laws to promote improvements in agriculture, commerce, industry, the "elegant arts," literature, and the sciences. His national wish list included an astronomical observatory and a national university. This Adams was a conservative in support of activist government, not an especially strange idea among conservatives in his time.

His commitment to the antislavery cause especially in the years after his presidency was hardly an exercise in conservative politics. Determined to continue a life of political action after his defeat by Andrew Jackson in 1828, he won a seat in the House of Representatives in 1830. He served there for the next 17 years, playing an important role in the antislavery movement, especially by fighting the "gag rule" in Congress, which automatically prevented the discussion of antislavery petitions. He also opposed the annexation of Texas and the Mexican War, which, like many of his fellow New Englanders, he interpreted as actions in support of the continuation and expansion of slavery. Like his father before him, John Quincy Adams could navigate between a commitment to solid conservative principles and the need to make reasonable adjustment to the needs of a growing democracy and the demands of a changing modern world.

By the time Andrew Jackson was inaugurated in 1829, the struggle to eliminate property qualifications for voting was already over in most states. The new states of the Northwest Territory (Ohio, Indiana, Illinois, Michigan, and Wisconsin) provided for universal manhood suffrage when they joined the union in accordance with the Northwest Ordinance shaped by Jefferson. Under pressure from those examples, other states soon followed suit in eliminating property qualifications for voting. Only Yankee Rhode Island and John Calhoun's South Carolina resisted. Riding the wave of egalitarian sentiment, more public offices were open to election by popular vote. American conservatives in the first half of the nineteenth century resisted the inexorable movement toward universal male suffrage. They mistrusted the growing urban masses and clung to the idea that property ownership should be tied to voting because society should be led by men who had a material stake in it. Locked into pre–Civil War conservative thought was the fear of the tyranny of the majority as the Republic grew more democratic and growing majorities were less representative of the propertied and the "natural aristocracy." Conservatives of the era like Chancellor James Kent of New York and Philadelphia banker Nicholas Biddle believed that democracy was a danger to property, and so they opposed the expansion of voting rights. They were, of course, wrong in their fears. Even as this age of reform separated suffrage from property holding, nevertheless, property remained secure from any assaults by the masses.

Andrew Jackson stands as another example of the difficulty of pigeonholing liberals and conservatives in this era. Jackson was a states' rights Democrat who nevertheless used the power of the federal government to limit the extraordinary influence of the Second National Bank of Nicholas Biddle on the national economy, and he succeeded in blocking its recharter. The Jacksonians presented themselves as defenders of equal opportunity, resisting the growing tendency of capital to encourage monopoly and limit competition. By adopting such a policy they encouraged the multiplication of state banks and new enterprises, not unhelpful to capital formation. The Jacksonian Democrats subscribed to Jefferson's cautions about the dangers of too strong a national government, but as president, Jackson used and enlarged the powers of his office in fighting the bank and in smashing South Carolina's self-indulgent nullification cabal. Jackson also broadened access to government service. Enemies accused Jackson of inventing the spoils system, but he replaced no higher a percent of federal employees than had Jefferson. This was a process that accompanied a shift of parties in power, practiced by both parties, and not an inherently corrupt practice. It brought new blood into government and opened office holding to more than just the elite. Historians have dubbed this the "age of the common man." It was a time when conservatives were on the defensive.

Daniel Webster, a more agile thinker than most conservatives of his day, acknowledged the risks to property in a broadly democratic polity, but his solution favored encouraging a wider distribution of property among the enfranchised. Webster, in tune with the thought of John Adams, made adjustments for a new era. He agreed that the propertied, who have a greater stake in the stability of society, should govern. But property broadly, even if modestly, held would benefit all. Proper interpretation of the Constitution, which he revered, would protect property and check popular excesses. Clearly, pre–Civil War conservatives associated property with freedom and feared that too much democracy endangered both. They tended to see the possession of property as a sign of personal merit. The success of the nation was dependent on a successful economy and the security of property.

Webster's view of government differed from those held by conservatives of Calhoun's stripe. He conceded an important role for a central government in an increasingly complex society of varied interests. As with Hamilton, government action to aid and stimulate business activity did not violate his conservative instincts. His habits of thought, while flexible at times, nevertheless insisted that religion, morality, and education should guide society. Conservatives like Webster rejected Hamilton's vision of a society embedded in class conflict in favor of recognizing a community of interest and mutual dependence between the business and laboring classes.[4]

One is impressed but not surprised by the nuances and variety of thought among conservatives of the first half of the nineteenth century. A rapidly changing society stimulated different ideas even among the similarly disposed. Sometimes shifting views resided in the same mind. Orestes Brownson, New England intellectual and eccentric, vacillated in his thought, embracing liberal and conservative views at different times. There were moments in his life when he recoiled from egalitarian democracy, others when he endorsed democratic ideas. He could not shake the view that people were fallible individually and collectively and could easily corrode the process of government. Like many conservatives he saw the need for authoritative government, yet he feared executive power in government and looked to the legislative branch to provide protection and restraint. His common tie to the conservative thought of his day was his emphasis on duty, authority, moral law, and the guidance of religion. Brownson also grew tired of the democratic rhetoric in praise of liberty and the rights of man and expressed his conservative instincts: "it's high time to hear something of the duties of men and the rights of authority."[5]

A Democrat of a different disposition added his voice to early American conservatism. John Calhoun was the South's leading champion of minority rights, states' rights, and limits to the power of the central government. That ideological posture he put to the very practical purpose of defending human slavery. In character and purpose, Calhoun's conservatism dictated deep distrust of and aversion to a powerful national government. In 1828 his ideas were gathered in the *South Carolina Exposition and Protest* detailing his doctrine of nullification of federal laws. Calhoun proposed that the individual states have the authority to declare federal legislation null within their borders. Had they been successful, John Calhoun and his allies would have given individual states effective veto power over national legislation. The immediate issue was a matter of federal tariff law imposing taxes on imports. Agrarians saw such taxes as a burden on rural America, especially in the South, for the benefit of emerging industries, especially in the North. But looming over Calhoun's nullification doctrine was the matter of slavery and Southern agrarian survival. What he propounded as a matter of protecting the rights of a minority was specifically aimed at protecting the peculiar institution of a minority section of the country. His aversion to a powerful national government was not, then, out of fear that a repressive government would trample the rights of free citizens, but that a national majority might one day move to free human beings from slavery. Calhoun stood for individualism, limited government, and states' rights to defend against abolitionist assaults on slavery and, incidentally, in defense of order and tradition. Inequality of wealth he saw as a natural product of a free society. As a representative of the minority South, he deeply distrusted majority rule, and his thrust in the nullification controversy was directed at safeguarding the interests of the South in the face of an expanding free-soil North and West. To this end he developed the idea of a "concurrent majority," intended to give the South a veto power over national policy. He dreamed that agreement among the three major sections of the country, North, South, and West, would be necessary for important national action. Calhoun reached back to an earlier political era to forge an alloy of states' rights theories because of his profound suspicions about popular majority rule that had also troubled the Federalists. His loathing of industrialism and his passionate defense of a slave-holding culture made for a conservatism of a distinctive cast. His ideas, in the end, served a secession movement dedicated to the "conservative" cause of preserving the institutions and the established social order dedicated to human bondage.

In the early decades of the American national experience, the attitude of conservative thinkers toward business enterprise was a mixed bag. Many, like Hamilton, Webster, and John Quincy Adams, saw the wisdom of government action to encourage industry for national prosperity and stability. Others harbored no clear antibusiness prejudice but retained a suspicion that excessively close ties between business and government would result in too much growth in government authority. Conservatives applauded business and economic success, but so, too, did most of their liberal friends. Much of the difference between liberal and conservative in relation to business enterprise had to do with emphasis and timing, and none of these differences prevented political cooperation on many issues. One of the clearer differences between liberals and conservatives on business issues concerned tariffs on imported goods. In the Jacksonian era, Democrats held to the Jeffersonian stand in favor of low tariffs; the more business-friendly Whigs supported business demands for higher tariffs to protect against foreign competition and to increase profits. Clearly, laissez-faire economic ideas were not yet fully embraced even by the business community. Americans, both conservative and liberal, who were dedicated to agrarianism were wary of the new industrialism with its potential to raise the prices of manufactured goods through protective tariffs and to lower prices for agricultural goods by market manipulation.

Conservatism, then, in the first half of nineteenth-century America was still principally devoted to the idea of preserving a stable society informed by religion and moral values and supportive of freedom in a republican nation. But religious Americans displayed a mix of conservative and reformist impulses. Americans in the early republic were intensely religious, in part because of the influence of the Second Great Awakening. From the 1790s and for decades that followed, religious revivalism stimulated great growth in American churches, multiplied denominations, and encouraged religious fervor. These developments bolstered conservative sentiment especially concerning religion and morals, but at the same time they also spawned an era of social reform, including movements for women's rights, education reform, prison reform, communal experiments, and especially the antislavery movement. That reform impulse, quickly embraced by liberals, soon gave many conservatives pause.

This was a generation that could recall the damage done by the European experience of ideology-driven revolutionary change without due respect for tradition, tempered reform, or responsive government. The development of American conservative ideas was shaped by an American experience that was very different from that of Europe. American conservatives were more clearly committed to republican government albeit with some cautions. A suspicion of the masses and the conviction that the propertied and well born should have a dominant role in government was shared by American conservatives, if less intensely than in Europe. Both sides of the Atlantic harbored a common disdain for the revolutionary ideas and excesses of the French experience. But the French Revolution was naturally much more traumatic for Europeans than for Americans, who witnessed the convulsions from afar. American conservatives, then, with appropriate cautions, were better able to accommodate to political and social change than conservatives in Europe.

It was the second half of the nineteenth century that witnessed the marriage of conservatism and capitalism, encouraged by a booming, large-scale industrialism and a growing materialist ethos. Some conservatives refused to attend the wedding. One who could not bless the union was an aging Henry Adams. In tune with family tradition, he distrusted democratic optimism and understood human nature to be seriously flawed. He also distrusted the tawdry materialism of the new corporate plutocracy. Early in the twentieth century in his meditations in *The Education of Henry Adams*, he looked back on the changes in American capitalist structures since 1840 and saw them as "obnoxious because of their vigorous and unscrupulous energy. They were revolutionary, troubling all the old conventions and values. . . . They tore society to pieces and trampled it under foot." Henry Adams rejected the idea that the new industrial world brought progress. He feared that corporations "swaying power such as has never in the world's history been trusted in the hands of private citizens . . . will ultimately succeed in directing the government itself." The future would suggest his fears were not unjustified. "The corporation is in its nature a threat against the popular institutions spreading so rapidly over the world. [U]nless some satisfactory solution of the problem can be reached, popular institutions may yet find their existence endangered."[6]

Henry Adams grew increasingly pessimistic about the future of the United States and the world. Even while he enjoyed the fruit of his own investments in modern enterprise, he could not judge the dynamic energy of the new capitalism as positive. His was a much darker vision of the future. He railed against a materialist, power-obsessed capitalism as a danger to civilization. He warned against the cheapening of the culture by increasingly self-centered individualism and materialism. When his investments suffered losses following the crash of 1894, Adams raged against the "rottenness of our whole social, industrial, financial and political system." His investments recovered, but by the end of the decade, he concluded that the United States had surrendered to the interests of finance capitalism, and American politicians were acting as servants under the command of big business. Here was a conservative mind that saw the new capitalism as a very unconservative force. But his doubts and critiques could not convert Adams into a reformer. Indeed, Adams reserved some of his sharpest barbs for the new-born reformist impulses of his friend Theodore Roosevelt. An emerging progressivism did not impress.

Of the forces of reform gathering behind Roosevelt, "one knew little; their cohesion was slight; their training irregular; their objects vague."[7]

Henry's brother, Brooks, shared his gloom and denounced the finance capitalists with a bitter invective more appropriate to Karl Marx than to an Adams scion. But Brooks, unlike his brother, applauded Theodore Roosevelt's efforts to enact regulatory measures during his presidency and approved of his strongly reformist platform in the 1912 presidential campaign. In that election Roosevelt set out a platform agenda that was pro-labor and promised to build on the program of business regulation he began while he was president. Capitalism was a system, Brooks agreed, that sacrificed all else to the making of money and needed restraint and policing. The modern capitalist "conceives sovereign powers to be for sale. He may, he thinks, buy them; and if he buys them; he may use them as he pleases." "He may sell his service to whom he pleases at what price may suit him, and if by doing so he ruins men and cities, it is nothing to him. He is not responsible, for he is not a trustee of the public. If he is retrained by legislation, that legislation is in his eye an oppression and an outrage, to be annulled or eluded by any means which will not lead to the penitentiary." He saw the capitalist as a revolutionary without knowing it. The capitalist "looks upon the evasion of a law devised for public protection, but inimical to him, as innocent or even meritorious." The capitalist class nurtured a "universal contempt for the law, and found judicial vetoes of legislative attempts to regulate capital a useful way to escape the reach of the law." He recognized the captive nature of the judicial system, noting that "[C]apitalists have usually been able to select the magistrates who decide their causes, perhaps directly through the intervention of some president or governor whom they have nominated by a convention controlled by their money." He feared that the federal courts, including the Supreme Court, were converted into tools of capital dedicated to protecting the interests of wealth. This is a thought that recurs in the American experience.

Brooks Adams believed the governing class had obligations to society, but the capitalist could not meet those obligations, especially the duty to uphold the law as a model to others in society. He recognized the developing power of plutocracy capable of reshaping society for its own benefit, and for a solution he looked to the growth of federal authority as a countervailing power.[8]

The voices of Henry and Brooks Adams were not radical. These men were the heirs to a long history of Adams family tradition honoring conservative values and democratic government responsible to public rather than private interests. There is more than a suggestion here that conservatives should have been wary of the disruptive and corrupting forces of the new capitalism, but this was not to be. During the last decades of the nineteenth century, most conservatives fell in line to support the kind of capitalist development that scorned government oversight, justified the manipulation of the law, and generated a set of materialist values grossly inappropriate for a genuinely conservative vision of society. This was the work of the Gilded Age.

3

Robber Barons, Darwin, and the Theft of Conservatism

The independent corporations of modest size that gave birth to the Industrial Revolution in America eventually succumbed to the age of the manipulative Robber Barons and giant monopolies after the Civil War. In this transformation the very nature of capitalism changed. So too did the uneasy relationship between capitalism and conservatism. The business classes in early America possessed a natural affinity for the conservative values of social stability and civic responsibility. They looked to government to sustain good order, and they welcomed economic protection and support as well. In the second half of the nineteenth century, the business attitude toward government changed sharply and so did the definition of conservatism for the business community. The new and massively expansive capitalism generated great innovations in business practices and a strong emphasis on corporate growth, both of which proved to be careless of tradition, indifferent toward religion, and little concerned with cultural stability. Capitalism now hammered out a new program for conservatism that was deeply disturbing to the traditionalist conservative thinkers of the age, a program that has distorted and confused conservative values ever since.

Rapid industrialization was well under way in America before the Civil War. The Industrial Revolution introduced the factory age beginning in New England and spreading to other northern states. Most businesses were of relatively small scale, locally owned, and owner managed. These conditions changed dramatically with the emergence of railroads and other large-scale enterprises, and the changes intensified rapidly after the Civil War. The success of American enterprise produced huge capital resources in the United States and attracted great sums of European money for investment in large-scale ventures. The railroad age and the successful exploitation of electricity and petroleum created giant corporations, absentee owned through shares of stock, managed by hired professionals, and staffed by a constant flow of immigrants and agrarians displaced by an increasingly mechanized agriculture. The new system succeeded wonderfully and produced unimagined wealth, and with that wealth, unprecedented power for the capitalist. The most ambitious moved beyond the operation of gigantic industrial corporations to building banking and financial structures that controlled multiple corporations and whole industries. Moneyed interests dominated the nation's political machinery as never before and set the direction for both business and government. The resulting free-wheeling capitalism was not reluctant to corrupt legislators at every level of government to help build ever greater fortunes. This was the Gilded Age.

The ever more dramatic industrial expansion and the enormous profits that came soon after the Civil War altered the character of American capitalism and the nation's politics. J. P. Morgan, John D. Rockefeller, Andrew Carnegie, and other business barons crafted the great industrial trusts. These monopolies built fabulous wealth, and that wealth generated economic and political power in private hands unimaginable only a few decades earlier.

In the 1870s the new oil-refining industry was intensely competitive. In keeping with capitalist lore, competition kept prices down and profit margins modest. John D. Rockefeller had a better idea. He engineered a collection of over 70 competing refineries into a single trust company. With the combined strength thus gathered, the Standard Oil Trust promptly bought up or forced out of business much of the remaining competition. By the time Rockefeller completed this process he controlled 95 percent of the oil-refining industry in the United States. This horizontal trust, one that monopolized all of one phase of production, succeeded so well it gave Rockefeller the resources to build a vertical trust combining his control of refining with investment in wells, rail transport, wholesale distribution, and retail outlets. He was able in this way to dominate oil production from source to final sale. Rockefeller's model was imitated in other major industries like railroads, steel, meat packing, and tobacco, turning the last decades of the nineteenth century into the age of monopoly. Public concern pressed Congress to pass the Sherman Anti-trust Act in 1890, but the law proved impotent against trusts and was invoked more often against labor unions than the monopolies that had inspired its passage. Businessmen continued to pay verbal tributes to the benefits of competition while they worked with untiring diligence to eliminate it.

One of the genuine rags-to-riches stories of the Gilded Age (they were not common) belonged to Andrew Carnegie. With his impoverished family he emigrated from Scotland to the United States as a young boy in 1848. At 14 he found work with the Pennsylvania Railroad, lived frugally, and saved and invested what he could. Through a series of shrewd business maneuvers he carved a place for himself in the rapidly expanding iron industry at a time when railroad expansion and bridge building in the United States created fabulous demand. His journey from mere success to industrial dominance was spurred by his pioneering adoption of the new Bessemer process in steel making, which generated a superior product. His organizing skill also constructed a vertical industrial structure that included all the production elements from ore fields, coal mines, and transportation to finished steel products. Years before the end of the century, Carnegie Steel enjoyed a near-complete monopoly of the industry.

Rockefeller and Carnegie were exceptional but not alone in the transition to trust/monopoly capitalism. Leaders in most major industries followed the pattern with great success, and the corrupting influence on the economic and political system was unrelenting. That set the stage for the next leap from mega industrial corporations to still more powerful finance capitalism whose leading architects were Rockefeller and J. P. Morgan.

By the approach of the twentieth century, Carnegie had accumulated so much money from his monopoly that he decided to retire and spent the rest of his life giving much of it away. He sold Carnegie Steel to J. P. Morgan, who combined it with a few remaining independent steel producers to create the United States Steel Corporation, the first company worth more than $1 billion. In 1900 dollars, that was impressive, but it was even more impressive when one considered that this was merely a sideline for Morgan, who also controlled a vast financial empire. By then the primary interests of people like Morgan and Rockefeller were in banking, through which they controlled dozens of corporations in industries like steel, oil, railroads, shipping, insurance, and other banks. In 1913, the Pujo Committee of the House of Representatives conducted an investigation of the banking industry in the United States. The committee discovered that banks controlled by Morgan and Rockefeller and two other banking houses in New York City dominated industries valued at over $45,000,000,000. Impressive in any age, but stunning in an age when a dollar was, for some, a day's pay.

More important than the money was the power it generated. The power that accompanied such wealth presented a challenge to democracy itself. In 1894 President Grover Cleveland faced the prospect of default by the U.S. government as a result of collapsing tax revenues during a prolonged economic depression. The government's resources were limited because income taxes were not permitted before the adoption of the Sixteenth Amendment, and excise tax and tariff revenue were inadequate. Unable to resolve the crisis for lack of public confidence in government bonds issued to raise money, Cleveland turned to J. P. Morgan, whose bank floated a bond issue on behalf of the U.S. Treasury. Investors with more confidence in Morgan than the U.S. government bought the bonds, the crisis was resolved, and incidentally the House of Morgan made a handsome multimillion-dollar commission for its services to the nation. To those who would notice, the episode revealed that Morgan commanded more economic power than the government itself. There was an important question here about the very nature of democracy. What was the significance of the electoral system if important matters of public policy that affected the lives of millions of people were decided not in state or national legislatures, but in the board rooms of giant corporations and banking houses? Most American conservatives, a few like the Adams brothers excepted, did not seem unduly concerned. Something about conservatism had changed.

Meanwhile, bribery and scandal at every level of government infected the American democracy. When the crimes were too flagrant to ignore, sporadic prosecution sent politicians, from city officials to presidential cabinet members, to jail. Meanwhile the bribe-doling capitalists generally escaped without penalty. With great eloquence some American writers like Henry George, Frank Norris, Ida Tarbell, and Upton Sinclair lamented the materialism, mechanization, and corruption of American society that accompanied expansive capitalist power in the nineteenth century, but with little effect on conservative thought.

The ingenuity of the more sophisticated business moguls went beyond blatant corruption to the manipulation of the law and the Constitution itself. The smooth operation of the new industrial/finance capitalism demanded liberating changes in the law, and the judicial system was ready enough to read the law in ways supportive of capital. Judges regularly rose from the ranks of corporate law and needed little prodding to offer sympathetic interpretations of state and federal statues and constitutional law with dramatic and permanent benefits to big business. Expense was no barrier; the most skilled lawyers stood ready to serve, and a pliant judiciary proved receptive to persuasion.

Two key changes molded legal interpretations to the service of the new capitalism. First, the American courts granted business corporations the status of persons under the law, and then they reshaped the judicial understanding of due process to protect entrepreneurs from even the most modest efforts at public oversight. In 1886 in the case of *Santa Clara County v. Southern Pacific Railroad Co.*, the Supreme Court accepted the interpretation of the word "persons" in the Fourteenth

Amendment as applying to corporations as legal "persons." This was not the intention of the framers of the amendment, but this ingenious twist of meaning proved a great boon to corporations. They were now entitled to the same rights as citizens to due process, and, in a series of cases, the court interpreted the phrase "due process" very generously. These were hardly strict constructionist or cautiously conservative readings of the Constitution.

The Fourteenth Amendment to the Constitution provides that no state shall "deprive any person of life, liberty, or property, without due process of law; nor deny to any person within its jurisdiction the equal protection of the laws." In a step more suggestive of imagination than logic, the courts began to apply the word "person" to corporations. During the Reconstruction period after the Civil War, the framers of the amendment had designed the amendment to provide citizenship and equality before the law to the recently freed, formerly slave population. The amendment was a commitment of the Northern states to equality of citizenship, and it served as a test of Southern willingness to cooperate in the Reconstruction process. It was not intended to insulate business corporations from government regulation.

The first serious efforts at business regulation of increasingly large and powerful corporations came at the state-level western state legislatures, pressured by their farm populations, acted against the exploitative practices of the railroads. The Supreme Court at first rejected this broader application of "person" to corporations in the Slaughter House Cases in 1873. But in cases rising from the Granger Laws of mid-western states regulating railroads, the court did accept the interpretation that corporations were persons under the meaning of the amendment. Finally in 1886 in the case of *Santa Clara County v. Southern Pacific Railroad*, the court even refused to hear arguments challenging the interpretation. Senator Roscoe Conkling of New York, a faithful friend of capital, claimed that Congress did intend the Fourteenth Amendment to protect corporations and misquoted the journal of the drafting committee to make it appear so. Beyond that distortion, one searches in vain for evidence that the framers of the Fourteenth Amendment had given any thought to providing a shield of legal protection to corporations. The result of the court's interpretation was the most beneficent application of restrictions against public regulation of corporations. That twisted interpretation survives into the twenty-first century to shackle attempts to regulate corporate abuses. A more precise and historically accurate reading of the Fourteenth Amendment would have revolutionary impact in limiting the often pernicious influence of big capital.[1]

A second judicial innovation revised the meaning of the words "due process" in the Constitution in another successful ploy to benefit corporate interests. The traditional understanding of due process applied the term to legal procedure. The government had to respect the prescribed process in passing, broadcasting, and enforcing a law or its legal impact against a person was rendered null. In the Dred Scott Case of 1857, Chief Justice Roger B. Taney argued that efforts to keep slavery out of the territories of the United States were unconstitutional because owners had a "vested right" in their slave property. His intention here was to declare that laws that barred owners from bringing their "property" into free territory *automatically* violate due process. Such laws were null even if mechanical procedures in passing, promulgating, and enforcing laws against slavery in the territories (and possibly, it was feared, even in the free states) were properly executed. With this decision by the Taney court, the slope toward Civil War became more slippery. In the longer run, the logic of the decision proved exceptionally convenient for corporate lawyers.

Stephen J. Field was a pro-Union Democrat from California appointed to the Supreme Court in 1863. Field saw himself as a guardian of property rights. He seized on Taney's vested rights idea, and after a long struggle with dissenters on the court, he finally succeeded in persuading the court to abandon a strictly procedural interpretation of due process in favor of the concept of "substantive" due process. By 1898 in the case of *Smyth v. Ames*, Field convinced the court that the due process clause, even if there were no defect in procedure in the passage and enforcement of the law, restricted the power of the state to interfere with a person's (i.e., a corporation's) property rights. The court decided that the railroad rates set by Nebraska law were not reasonable, and as such constituted a violation of due process. Thus, any law the effect of which reduced a corporation's profits could be judged as a violation of property rights and therefore rendered unconstitutional. Once the court established the precedent, this strained interpretation of the due process clause stood as a bulwark against government regulation of business enterprise. In this way the court narrowly defined the police power of government and severely restricted it to matters that directly affected public health, safety, and morals. The court assumed for itself the power to judge what was fair and what was unfair in economic regulation under the veil of this novel constitutional interpretation with no real connection to the intention of the framers.

Before the Civil War the Supreme Court recognized broad powers of government to regulate the activities of corporations in the public interest. Granting corporations the constitutional status of persons and broadening the barriers to state regulation through the application of substantive due process were novel and unwarranted interpretations of the Constitution for the obvious benefit of capital. These new decisions immunized corporations from effective state or federal oversight and cleared the way for the unrestrained exploitation of labor, the consumer, and even the unwary small investor. Here was a key moment in the establishment of American laissez-faire economic practice. Now unrestricted free enterprise had the support of the judicial system, and under the law, private economic interests took precedence over the needs of the society, a condition hardly compatible with traditional conservative standards.

During the twentieth century, conservatives often insisted on a narrow interpretation of the Constitution with strict adherence to the intention of the framers as far as it could be known. This was true especially as applied to laws that benefited the unions and the working class. Such was not the attitude on behalf of capital in the age of the moguls. Elastic interpretations placed the courts at the service of big business.

Hostility to government regulation of corporations persisted in the judicial system and especially in Supreme Court decisions until a more liberal legal philosophy emerged with judicial appointments by presidents Roosevelt, Truman, Eisenhower, Kennedy, and Johnson. But in the closing decades of the twentieth century new appointees by presidents Nixon, Reagan, and Bush restored the defense of laissez-faire to legal reasoning. Justices William Rehnquist, Sandra Day O'Connor, Antonin Scalia, Anthony Kennedy, and Clarence Thomas were consistently unfriendly to federal regulation and favored passing more power to the states except when states tried to enact laws to regulate business. In more recent years, the court has struck down all significant restraint on campaign contributions, enabling conservative political action committees and corporations to pour obscene amounts of money into the political process in defense of corporate freedom of speech, a right of "persons" under the Constitution. There is power in that money to corrupt the democracy itself. Such is the inheritance of Gilded Age jurisprudence, and oddly, conservatives witness and applaud.

The colossal growth in the wealth and influence of American capitalists was assisted not only by a friendly judiciary. The development of religious and pseudoscientific theories well suited to the needs of the business community also offered generous support. Armed with innovative judicial theory, the ideas of Social Darwinism, and the preaching of the Gospel of Wealth, the capitalist establishment recast traditional conservative ideology to the service of free enterprise.

In the process core conservative values were muted or offered as mere lip service. Embracing these legal, social, and doctrinal convictions, the Gilded Age consummated the shotgun marriage of conservatism and capitalism, a match that could not have been blessed by classic conservatives.

In 1859 Charles Darwin published *On the Origin of Species*, and the understanding of the natural world forever changed. It has been said that Darwin did for biology what Einstein was soon to do for physics. The theory of evolution based on natural selection within species whose members competed for scarce resources was such a dynamic and exciting idea that it quickly spilled outside the field of biology and into the social sciences, a flow unintended by Darwin and short on evidence. The mutation of evolution theory into social, economic, and political theory opened a whole new world of speculation about the nature of society. In economic and social science, a grand structure of ideas was built with parts that seemed to fit neatly together—except for a weak and unsubstantial foundation. Darwin's idea of evolution was based on scientific biological evidence. In a world of limited resources, individuals of a species struggled to survive. If particular individuals were born with a trait that helped in the struggle, they were favored to survive. If that trait came from a genetic change, it passed on to the next and future generations. The evidence for genetic mutation was yet to be discovered, and the precise mechanism of inherited traits was unknown to Darwin. But from his field studies, he correctly concluded that a sufficient number of such changes could result in the emergence of new species and could thus explain the process of evolution from simple to more complex organisms. Great scientific and especially religious controversy followed the publication of *On the Origin of Species*. The scientific community quickly embraced the theory, and some religious denominations adapted. Others stood stubbornly hostile and remain so to this day. The influence of this new idea of evolution was quick and powerful. It spawned a Social Darwinism that simply transposed biological science to social science by acts of will and imagination, but without adequate scientific justification. Once the initial leap was taken and the assumed foundation laid, the rest of the structure grew rapidly even if it lacked logical stability.

The timing of Social Darwinism was perfect for an age of enterprise looking to justify laissez-faire economics. It provided a convenient and, for the receptive, a persuasive explanation for wealth, for poverty, and for the triumph of monopoly and finance capitalism. The theory also bolstered the proposition that the system should not be tampered with by an intrusive government infected with sentimental ideas about providing for the general welfare. The argument was straightforward even if erroneous in its first premise. The key words for Social Darwinists were *competition* and *struggle*. As in biological life, survival and success in social life were difficult and full of obstacles. Competition and struggle created a kind of natural selection whereby the able, the intelligent, and the talented survived and prospered; in short, the very competitive nature of social life assured the survival of the fittest. The conclusion easily followed that those at the top of the social ladder, the successful and the wealthy, were self-evidently the most fit. Economic success and social standing were simply assumed to be the unchallenged standards of "fitness." Those who were poor and stayed poor were the unfit, and over the decades and centuries the pitiless struggle would sadly but inevitably weed them out. As biological life was often brutal, "red in tooth and claw" in Tennyson's phrase, so, too, social life was full of hardship and dangers. The struggle was painful, but such was the natural order of things, and the natural order must be allowed to function for the long-term progress of society. To interfere with this natural process by artificial social reforms could only slow the advance of society. This was a hard doctrine, but its advocates insisted that the alternative to the survival of the fittest was the continued reproduction and survival of the unfit. Only in the long, slow run of evolution would society gradually improve and perfect itself through struggle, so long as there was no intrusion to upset the natural process, especially intrusion by government.

If an individual were among the fit, poverty for that person should only be a temporary condition, perhaps the product of circumstance or bad luck. According to the reigning philosophy, the fit would rise above the difficulty and eventually prosper. If poverty persisted, the sad conclusion was unavoidable. There was hope. Intelligence, energy, and a strong will could carry one out of poverty to success and prosperity. This idea, imaginatively captured in the popular Horatio Alger stories, fed the myth of rags to riches. Such a climb was possible, as in the case of Andrew Carnegie, but his experience was exceptional. Most of the business bigwigs of the Gilded Age and ever since were born to prosperous families, a condition of measurable advantage in the business world. Rags, in fact, usually remained tattered, not from inbred unfitness, but from the social and economic realities of an unresponsive system.

The phrase "survival of the fittest" is attributed not to Darwin but to the British sociologist Herbert Spencer. Writing in biology and philosophy, Spencer drew a huge audience on both sides of the Atlantic. Though not university trained, he was one of the leading scholars in the field of sociology when that discipline was in its formative beginnings. Darwin's work provided Spencer with a scientific patina for thought he had already formed concerning society and the human struggle for survival. He embraced the idea that positive social change could not come quickly, but only after long ages of struggle. By the middle of the nineteenth century, economic and scientific progress had indeed improved social conditions for millions, especially in the Western world. That progress was the product of ages of struggle and competition among human beings. The Western world was in better condition than it had ever been, and in the future it would be better than it was then. The theory held that war and natural calamity might produce reversals, but, however tragic, these were temporary setbacks and could be overcome. The evident trend of social evolution was toward progress. That progress was the result of competition and must be allowed to proceed on its own course at its own pace. To interfere with social evolution by government regulations or worse, by utopian socialist schemes, would only interfere with and damage the progress of society. Whatever human cost social evolution exacted was the regrettable but unavoidable price of long-term progress.

Spencer announced these brutal dicta without apology. He rejected government assistance for the poor, who were the unfit; better for society that they should die away. For Spencer the function of government was simply to maintain law and order. (Why violence and crime should not also be part of the natural process of competition, he did not effectively address, though the achievement of wealth and high social standing by fraud and other crimes was not unknown.) There ought to be no government role in providing for or overseeing education, housing conditions, tariffs, banking, medical practice, or even the mail. For Spencer evolution pointed to the desirability of laissez-faire individualism, and government or collective social action violated natural law.

William Graham Sumner, deeply influenced by Spencer's thought, became the leading proponent of Social Darwinism in America. He joined the faculty at Yale University in 1868, became professor of political and social science in 1872, and spent much of the rest of his career promulgating the doctrine of the survival of the fittest. For Sumner an understanding of evolution made the idea of equality ridiculous. Evolutionary struggle led some men to accumulate great wealth, and wealth was the mark of success and fitness. He once wrote, "The aggregation of large amounts of capital in few hands is the first condition of the fulfillment of the most important tasks of civilization which now confront us."[2] Natural selection produced millionaires. Becoming wealthy provided a service to society, and no impediments should stand in the way of such ambition, certainly not the interference of government regulations or the quack schemes of reformers. Sumner was consistent in his application of laissez-faire theory. He was unalterably opposed to protective tariffs, a function of government that the business community continued to smile on, indeed, to insist upon. He subscribed to the full creed of the Social Darwinist faith. His prescription posited the fullest liberty, inequality, and the survival of the fittest, and rejected restraint, equality, and the survival of the less well endowed. Social progress depended on the first set. Society should be passive in the face of evolutionary struggle so that the talented could rise to dominance, and the weak would gradually die off. The function of the state was simply to maintain good order and do little else. In economics, progress, the advance of civilization, and positive human development depended in the long run on the energy and talent of individuals and the brute struggle of the market. Conservative businessmen applauded Sumner, but if he were to be considered a conservative, one had to account for certain distortions. He was impatient with tradition, skeptical in religion, and inclined to utilitarianism. His unshakable faith in the benefits of unrestrained capitalism did not fit classic conservative orthodoxy and contributed much to the distortion of American conservatism. (See Appendix A.)

Spencer and Sumner were greatly admired and widely read in the United States. The ideas of Social Darwinism dominated the work of university classrooms, newspapers, journals, lecture halls, and even many pulpits in the last quarter of the nineteenth century and beyond. But for some, including those committed to Protestant fundamentalism and the literal reading of Genesis, a social theory based on evolution was abhorrent. So for those who could not bow to Darwinism, biological or social, a set of religious ideas served to reach similar conclusions. Andrew Carnegie, himself, and a number of important Protestant ministers tried to reconcile the ideas of Spencer and Sumner with prevailing religious ideas to produce something called the Gospel of Wealth.

As noted, the life of Andrew Carnegie was one of the genuine rags-to-riches stories of the nineteenth century. From humble origins he built his empire in the steel industry, sold it to J. P. Morgan in 1900, and retired as one of the richest men in the world. While building that empire, he became a friend of Herbert Spencer and an enthusiastic supporter of his ideas. Generalizing from his own experience, Carnegie believed that wealth was the product of natural ability and energy, and that competition among the energetic was essential in life's struggles. He recognized that the law of competition could be brutal, but whether benign or not, "It is here; we cannot evade it; no substitutes have been found; and while the law may be sometimes hard for the individual, it is best for the race, because it insures the survival of the fittest in every department."[3] He believed that democracy and civilization itself depended on the protection of property and a successful capitalist system.

In 1889 Carnegie published an essay, "Wealth," in the influential *North American Review.* This was both a justification for the accumulation of great wealth and an admonition to the rich to avoid ostentation and waste and to do good deeds with their excess wealth. Reflecting his personal outlook, Carnegie combined Darwinian justifications of competition and wealth with the Christian duty to stewardship. Some of his colleagues of fulsome resources embraced the combination; many dropped the second clause. Carnegie was more consistent; after he withdrew from the steel industry, he spent much of the rest of his life giving many millions of dollars to communities and public institutions throughout the country.

For Carnegie, free enterprise and the goodwill of the rich were a necessary combination. If the laws of accumulation are left free, "individualism will continue, but the millionaire will be but a trustee for the poor, entrusted for a season with a great part of the increased wealth of the community, for administering it for the community far better than it could or would have done for itself." The thought is telling. Consciously or not, Carnegie here conceded that the entrepreneur's wealth was drawn from the community. But the community was not to be trusted to administer it; that should be the burden of the wiser minds that were able to extract the wealth. The rich man with surplus wealth becomes "the mere trustee and agent for his poorer brethren, bringing to their service his superior wisdom, experience, and ability to administer, doing for them better than they would or could do for themselves." "The gospel of wealth but echoes Christ's words," and for the rich man who gives his surplus wealth to his fellow men, "no bar will be found at the gates of Paradise."[4] Carnegie served as a kind of bridge between secular and religious justifications of free competition.

While Carnegie managed to combine Darwinian and Christian ideas, some believers, especially but not limited to those given to Bible inerrancy, were disturbed by this reliance on evolutionary theory, if not by the brutality of these economic doctrines. From them came a different but still capital-friendly response. Parallel to the development of Social Darwinism was the preaching of a more orthodox version of Gospel of Wealth that placed ideas similar to Carnegie's more firmly in a religious context and added to them. The Gospel of Wealth broadcast by the many preachers also carried with it an explanation for both wealth and poverty, but it made God responsible for both. Popular Christian preachers argued that government-sponsored economic and social legislation responding to the economic hardships of society should not interfere with God's will. This novel gospel message is evident in the words of Henry Ward Beecher, probably the most famous Protestant preacher of era: "God intended the great to be great and the little to be little." A dollar a day was sufficient even for a man with a family if he avoided drunkenness and waste, because "the man who cannot live on bread and water is not fit to live."[5]

Another influential preacher of the day, Russell Conwell, was a remarkable man. He was born to a farm family of modest means in Massachusetts and became a Baptist minister at the age of 37, an atheist convert to Christianity. After serving a church in Lexington, Massachusetts, he accepted a call to Philadelphia, where he built Grace Church into the largest Protestant church in the United States. With growing fame as a skilled preacher, he turned an inspirational lecture into a multimillion-dollar enterprise and used his money to found Temple University and served as the school's president. Conwell was the most successful preacher of the Gospel of Wealth. He taught his gospel lesson in a lecture entitled "Acres of Diamonds," which he delivered to rapt audiences over 6,000 times, accumulating several million dollars in fees in the process. The most quotable line in the address set the tone: "I say you ought to get rich, and it is your duty to get rich." He argued that 98 percent of rich men were honest and could be trusted to do good things with their money. One can do more good with money than without it, so the accumulation of wealth was not a selfish goal; it was a Christian duty. Money conferred power, and Christians ought to have it. Poverty was unfortunate, but not a matter of excessive concern. One should sympathize with the poor, but poverty was as inevitable as sin and largely the result of sin. "To sympathize with a man whom God has punished for his sins, thus to help him when God would still continue a just punishment is to do wrong." If the poor were the cause of their own poverty, government efforts to alleviate poverty would not be appropriate and would do little good. Like Carnegie, Conwell claimed a confident understanding of God's will, and that will should not be frustrated by futile government efforts to help the sinful poor. Enabling sin would only insure continuing poverty.[6]

With innovative theological language, the preachers of the Gospel of Wealth echoed the secular Social Darwinist justifications for wealth and poverty, combined with stern warnings against interference with natural evolution or God's will by damaging and foolish government action. This revised gospel required some neglect of a key teaching of traditional Christianity. In a kind of contorted Calvinism, these preachers developed a capitalist-friendly theory of election. The rich were God's chosen and appropriately blessed; poverty, if it persisted, was a product of sin and signaled God's displeasure. One wonders how these careful readers of scripture reconciled their exegesis with the Gospel of Mark 10:23, in which Jesus warns, "It is easier for a camel to pass through the eye of a needle than for a rich man to enter the kingdom of God." Even if "needle" (a narrow city gate) is taken only as metaphor, it is a hard passage for the rich to negotiate. The Gospel of Wealth interpretation of poverty must also have required some agility in skimming Luke 6:20, "Blessed are you who are poor, for the kingdom of God is yours."

The Gospel of Wealth and Social Darwinism neatly meshed on core issues. (1) Business enterprise should be allowed free action; progress demanded it; free competition would weed out the weak. (2) Political and social leadership should be left to a natural aristocracy, a sign of which was wealth. (3) The function of government should be limited to the protection of property and sustaining good order. (4) The rich are and ought to be the stewards of society. (5) Poverty is a badge of failure or sin, and the poor should accept the leadership of the wealthy.

Despite the stiff-necked confidence of the Social Darwinists and the righteous posturing of the Gospel of Wealth preachers, explaining the persistence of poverty in an age of growing prosperity and fabulous fortunes rested in something other than biological unfitness, sin, or God's wrath. Prevailing business practices of the Gilded Age *guaranteed* that most of the working class would live in or at the edge of poverty. Solid economic theory taught that raising wages cut into profits. No effort was spared, then, to keep wages as low as possible. Fierce hostility to unions, yellow-dog contracts, blacklisting, and the application of violence to strikebreaking were all employed with determined regularity to keep wages low and profits high. Streams of immigration provided the surplus labor so convenient to the business models of the day. Nevertheless, the combination of evolution theory applied to social science and the evocation of God's blessing on laissez-faire capitalism was powerfully persuasive to the generation of the Gilded Age. Nor has the attraction of those ideas entirely lost its grip on the American imagination. In recent decades echoes of the Gospel of Wealth lived on in the work of televangelists like Jerry Falwell and Pat Robertson. Their messages often tied faith, capitalism, and individual success and prosperity in a close bond. The wealthy are still widely admired as exemplars not only of success but also of virtue and intelligence, despite abundant evidence to the contrary. Nor has the idea that assistance to the poor is a waste of good money squandered on irresponsible recipients disappeared from polite society. "Welfare," "safety net," and "minimum wage" remain dirty words among most modern conservatives. The important impact of Social Darwinism and the Gospel of Wealth on conservative thought encouraged the broad embrace of an idea most welcome by big business: that government should be passive, especially in dealing with business enterprise, except perhaps for providing cash subsidies, protective tariffs, and stern police action against uppity unions.

The idea of government passivity in relation to business enterprise did not begin with the Social Darwinists or the Gospel of Wealth preachers. The phrase "laissez-faire" originated with a group of eighteenth-century French economists fighting the prevailing mercantilist restrictions on commerce. It came to be most directly associated with the ideas of Adam Smith in his work *The Wealth of Nations*. Also combating mercantilist ideas that prescribed detailed government regulations of commercial enterprise, Smith argued that competition in free markets with each entrepreneur pursuing his own advantage would ultimately result in the most efficient and productive exchanges to the greatest benefit of business, the consumer, and the economy of the nation. The invisible hand of competition governing supply and demand in a free market constituted the essential elements of economic success. This was a new and startling theory rising out of the last years of the Enlightenment, and it met stiff resistance even among many businessmen who preferred the benefits of government tariff protection, monopoly charters, and subsidies. But during the Gilded Age in America it became the new economic orthodoxy. Its disciples, however, spliced heretical ideas on to the purer doctrine of *Wealth of Nations* to shape an economic creed Smith would have rejected.

Adam Smith taught the benefits of laissez-faire economics could accrue only in a truly free market. This was an exceedingly elusive creature to capture. Smith saw the problem and warned that free markets could be distorted not only by government, but by entrepreneurs themselves. Business units that became too large (to say nothing about monopolies) or which conspired with competitors to influence prices or supplies would damage the free market and negate its benefits to society. Smith, in fact, saw an important role for government intervention to prevent such distortion of the market, a postulate unspoken among free-market partisans then and now. Incidentally, Smith also saw a necessary role for government in supporting infrastructure and other public works for the advantage of both business enterprise and the public. For those whose incomes benefited from works supported by the community, he suggested proportional income taxes, another prescription ignored by those who rely on a selective reading of *The Wealth of Nations.*[7] In the heyday of free enterprise capitalism, its defenders sang the praises of competition as a necessary element for economic progress, while its practitioners did all they could to kill competition and control markets. The laissez-faire advocates expressed carefully selected ideas drawn from Smith in the language science and religion to form a powerfully persuasive political outlook for conservative defenders of capital.

These business-friendly readings of science, religion, and economics, however, did not go entirely unchallenged. Counterarguments developed and used similar weapons, Darwinism and the Gospel, to offer an alternative vision of economic progress and social justice.

Darwinian influence was pervasive, but some progressives like sociologist Lester Ward offered a different adaptation of the idea of evolution. They too made the leap and accepted the idea that society evolved as biological life did. But they pointed out that evolution had finally produced an organism that understood the process. Why should humans sit passively watching evolution take its interminable and painful time to produce its advances? Since humans understood the process, why should they not intervene in it to produce a better result in shorter time? Using the metaphor of agriculture, they pointed out that farmers did not propagate plants and animals by setting them out in the wilderness hoping for a better breed to emerge from competition with other flora and fauna. They mitigated the waste of excessive struggle in favor of careful cultivation for healthier, more desirable specimens. Why then should not society intervene to mitigate the harsh conditions of capital markets and uncontrolled economics and take measures to improve public health and education and to reduce poverty? This Reform Darwinist outlook served as one justification for an emerging progressive or liberal approach to economics and politics in late nineteenth-century America. It served as a secular parallel to Social Darwinism and soon captured the imagination of progressive reformers.

As was the case with conservatives who did not like the evolutionary framework, progressives could also turn to religion. The Social Gospel emerged as the counterpoint to the Gospel of Wealth of Carnegie and Conwell. It developed from the preaching of a number of important Protestant ministers who worked among the laboring classes that faced the hardships of urban industrial life. Men like Washington Gladden and Walter Rauschenbusch worked among the poor and produced theological justifications for economic and social intervention on behalf of the working classes. As did the Reform Darwinists, the Social Gospel preachers looked to government as the agency that could effectively intervene against the brutality of current business practices. For Catholics, coincidental with the spread of the Social Gospel came the publication of the papal encyclical "Rerum Novarum" by Leo XIII in 1891. This too was a strong critique of unregulated capitalism and insisted on the rights of workers to safe working conditions, to join in unions, and to a living wage. The pope's message resonated among the heavily immigrant Catholic working class, and Catholic clergy like social activist monsignor John Ryan preached their own social gospel in tune with their protestant brothers.

Thus, in the last years of the nineteenth century, ideas emerged that formed the basic attitudes of conservatism and liberalism in American politics for the following century. Supporters of prevailing economic practices evoked the ideas of Social Darwinism or the Gospel of Wealth or both. Liberals drew from the thought of Reform Darwinism and the Social Gospel. From those beginnings, Americans have argued ever since about whether there has been too much or not enough government in the regulation of the economy and in providing economic security for all Americans. Sociologists no longer argue that social change replicates Darwinian biology, and for most people it is not fashionable to proclaim openly that poverty is God's punishment for sin. That thought, however, has not entirely disappeared from the more extreme rhetoric of the Right. The language and the rationale have changed, but many conservatives still embrace, to one degree or another, the attitudes rooted in Social Darwinism and the Gospel of Wealth. Wealth automatically signals intelligence and excellence even when produced by inheritance or chicanery; poverty is easily blamed on the poor. Belief in the progressive nature and beneficence of free-market competition that should not be tampered with by government survives as revered doctrine without serious challenge in conservative circles.

The Gilded Age celebration of the merger of the capitalist and the conservative obscured some very unconservative developments. The rapid, unplanned, and materialist-driven changes caused by the new capitalism did not generate alarm or even broad concern. Modern capitalism favored self-indulgence over restraint, as the keen social analyst Christopher Lash has pointed out, and its practitioners worked steadily and successfully "to create new demands and new discontents that can be assuaged only by the consumption of commodities."[8] Without effective protest from conservatives, pecuniary values supplanted more traditional values. Economic interests and economic power dominated the society. The wealthy and much of the middle class prospered, but the mere accumulation of wealth and the stimulation of material consumption had not been in the past the objectives of conservative ideology.

A few conservatives would not applaud, and, like the Adams brothers, they regretted the general embrace of materialist values without regard for their transforming influence on society. But most self-described conservatives accepted the new capitalist-defined standards for conservative thought. By 1920, classic conservatism was moribund in America; its few but stubbornly consistent adherents looked sadly on a culture that was now, in the words of Russell Kirk, "wholly subordinated to economic appetite." Conservative English critic Roger Scruton recently lamented the association of conservatism with a free-market economy and described the unregulated market as a generator of monopoly or oligarchy with power to rival the state.[9] The association of conservatism with the free market long predated Scruton's observation; the union was firmly set before the turn of the twentieth century. By the second half of the century, voices of classic conservatives like Kirk and Scruton were few and without measurable influence on conservative politics.

During the Gilded Age, capitalism kidnapped conservatism and sought no ransom.

4

Conservatives and Progressives Switch Horses

Darwinism and the Gospel of Wealth provided a defense of laissez-faire capitalism at a time when the abuses of the great corporations, the hardships of the working classes, and periodic economic depressions, as in the 1870s and 1890s, fired up calls for reform. At first, reformers focused on the problem of corporation-sponsored corruption. The Liberal Republican Movement in 1872 responded to corruption during the first Grant Administration by running a third-party ticket headed by journalist Horace Greeley. Charles Francis Adams, father of Henry and Brooks, led the race for the nomination for a time, but Greeley captured the Liberal Republican convention in Cincinnati and the nomination. Grant won a sweeping victory. He was still the popular hero of the Civil War, and the revelations of corruption on his watch were not yet fully enough exposed. In 1884 a group of Republican renegades dubbed the Mugwumps rejected the party's nominee, James G. Blaine, whose reputation was stained by suspicion of corrupt business dealings. They offered to vote for a Democrat if that party nominated an honest man. It was an offer the Democrats could not refuse, having failed to win the presidency in six consecutive elections. They chose Grover Cleveland, a New Yorker of impeccable reputation. The Mugwump defections were a factor in Cleveland's election. The Liberal Republican campaign and the Mugwump revolt were not programs seeking progressive reforms; they were significant anticorruption protests within the Republican Party. But corruption alone could not account for the suffering of so many American farmers, who worked hard but lived on the edge of poverty. Nor could corruption be blamed for the despair of those farmers who were forced to abandon their land to bank foreclosures and trudge to the cities in search of work. There they met others, many of them immigrants, in the search of jobs or already working for wages inadequate to support a family. Meanwhile the upper classes lived with scandalous opulence. Ugly as it was, corruption was not the cause of all this malaise.

Those with reforming inclinations gradually came to realize that the corruption of politicians was a symptom of problems that lay deeper, in the very structure of the economic system. The working classes could not identify corrupt political machines as the principal cause of their hardships when they suffered from low wages, poor sanitation, inadequate health care, and poor education. It took some time for progressive reformers to understand that the problems of urban corruption and poverty were connected and had to be addressed by government at the local and national levels. Influenced by ideas of Reform Darwinism and the Social Gospel, the progressive minded began to add to their anticorruption message a call to support the laboring masses, social legislation, educational reform, and restraints against the power and abuses of big business.

Proffered solutions varied. Small, Marxist-inspired socialist groups called for an end to capitalism itself, but they were never effective electoral threats in the United States. Few Americans listened to and fewer voted for socialist parties. In America radicalism simply did not appeal. Conservative politicians understood this and repeatedly tried to identify and label even moderate reformers as radicals.

In the 1990s the agrarian Populist Party translated the suffering of American farmers exploited by an age of expansive industrialism into a movement that won millions of votes. For a time, the party, formally titled the People's Party of the United States, controlled some state governments in the Midwest and was influential in others. The Populists were among the first reformers to see and proclaim the need for federal action to redress the economic imbalances of the nation. This was especially so after the courts crippled efforts at state regulation of railroads and other corporations. Organized as an active national party by 1892, the Populists nominated James B. Weaver for president, and their Omaha Platform called for important changes in the American economic and political system. The party demanded federal currency reform to fight deflation that depressed agricultural prices and drove millions of farmers off the land. Farmers had also suffered intensely from rate manipulation by railroads, and the most radical Populist proposal called for federal operation of the rail system. The platform also listed demands for the popular election of senators (still chosen then by state legislatures dominated by party bosses), provisions for initiative and referendum elections, and a graduated income tax. Conservatives regarded all these as radical ideas in 1892, but much of the platform list became law within 20 years. A young and still conservative Theodore Roosevelt read the Omaha Platform and concluded that the Populists would one day have to be confronted at the barricades. It was too soon for some of these ideas, but progressives, ironically including Roosevelt himself, would eventually catch up with and pass the Populists of 1892.

Meanwhile a movement of urban and state government reformers emerged calling themselves Progressives and moving beyond feeble anticorruption tactics. After repeated failures fighting corrupt political machines at the polls, they eventually learned that the electoral strength of those machines relied on effective organizing to harvest the support of the working classes and the urban poor. For the poor, the machine often served as the only social agency providing help in a society with no economic safety net of any kind. The answer to corrupt machines, these new Progressives realized, was to build well-organized, honest political machines. Among the most successful of the Progressives was Robert La Follette in Wisconsin. He rose to national prominence creating an honest machine and led a successful campaign for social reform. Winning the governorship after a long struggle against entrenched conservatives, he championed laws to control railroad rates, provision for a minimum wage, workmen's compensation for injuries, direct election of senators, and women's suffrage. Because of La Follette, what became known as the "Wisconsin Idea" served as a model for other Progressives. Such reform efforts were uniformly and strenuously opposed everywhere by the new conservatism, now fully dedicated to protecting the interests of capital.

Progressives, including both Democrats and Republicans, combined with many Populists after 1900 and looked increasingly to the federal government to address the economic and social injustices of the day. This bipartisan Progressive movement at the national level posed the first effective, if modest, political challenge to laissez-faire capitalism in America. The reformers drew from two of the same sources as the conservatives for inspiration: science and religion. As noted, Reform Darwinists argued for government intervention in social and economic affairs to produce speedier and more humane results than those in the brutal vision of Social Darwinism. Some reformers chose the religious arguments of the Social Gospel. Both Protestant and Catholic leaders advocated economic and social reforms that called for community action and government intervention to control the power of capital. Armed with such ideas, Progressives competed against the new, revisionist conservatism intent on the unqualified defense of a completely free enterprise system. Out of this confrontation came the twentieth-century political struggles between conservative and liberal approaches to modern capitalism. Both were committed to a capitalist economic system, but conservatism as a political ideology became increasingly defined and controlled by the demands of that system.

Ever since the days of his battles with John Adams and the Federalists, American conservatives disdained Thomas Jefferson and the ideological set that bore his name. Jeffersonianism expressed too much faith in the governing capacity of the common man, pushed hard for too broad an electorate, and overemphasized equality. Early conservatives did not share the Jeffersonian prejudice against a stronger national government, but rather insisted on authority effective enough to guarantee a well-ordered society. The rise of modern industrial and finance capitalism worked changes in political perspectives, particularly on the question of government powers, and eventually conservatives and liberals discovered they had switched sides on a key political outlook. As the forces of reform gathered in support of state and federal activism, the new capitalist conservatism took notice, and an odd reversal of rhetoric and rationalization took place. Like two travelers who unwittingly picked up each other's bags and boarded their separate trains, conservatives and liberals switched key ideas on government and politics. Liberals, who had long harbored Jeffersonian reservations about strong government, finally realized that the only force in society strong enough to challenge the power of self-serving capital was an effective national government. Conservatives, who had long insisted that security and good order required an authoritative government, now believed the least government was the best. When the twentieth century was still in its teens, reforming liberals looked to a stronger federal government to implement their agenda, and conservatives fully embraced the capitalist program that now called for a limited government staying off the backs of dynamic entrepreneurs. (Strong protective tariff legislation to bar foreign competition and police action against labor unions persisted as the unadvertised exceptions to restrained government.) In his thoughtful study of conservatism in America, historian Clinton Rossiter argued that when the new conservatism combined laissez-faire economics with Jeffersonian language, they abandoned the older conservative tradition.[1]

Progressives retained many of their Jeffersonian prejudices even if they now looked to a stronger federal government. They were, however, unimpressed by the Marxist ideas in circulation in the second half of the nineteenth century. They were firmly committed to capitalism as an economic system, but they were increasingly distressed by the corruption that seemed endemic in the age of the mogul. Even more worrisome was the enormous power exercised by these men, who, though not answerable to any electorate, could dominate and even reshape the society. That kind of private power threatened to make the democratic process meaningless. The great questions of national destiny were being answered not in the halls of government, but by private men in settings closed to public scrutiny. Beyond social reform, the key aim of Progressives was to restrain the power of big business and create a capitalist economy that was more humane, more just, and more responsive to a democratic electorate.

At the national level the struggle began in earnest with the administration of Theodore Roosevelt, an unlikely liberal given the ideological sympathies of his early career. Fiercely opposed to corruption, he championed civil service reform under Presidents Benjamin Harrison and Grover Cleveland. This was the start of a shift from his first political venture as a New York state assemblyman, when he opposed legislation friendly to labor and expressed little concern about the influence of capital. Yet even in his most conservative days, Roosevelt could be flexible and open minded. When he opposed state legislation to help New York City cigar makers in 1882, he accepted the invitation of union leader Samuel Gompers to tour the tenements where the work was done. Appalled that men, women, and children were forced to work in squalid conditions for the poorest wages, he reversed his stand and supported remedial legislation. His friendship with crusading journalist Jacob Riis and his stint as a New York City police commissioner also awakened Roosevelt to how the "other half" lived.

After his glory days, his "shining hour," in Cuba in 1898, New York rewarded her Rough Rider hero with election to the governorship. Rewarding heroism was not the pure motive of the Republicans who nominated him. In 1898 scandals had put the party's electoral chances in jeopardy. They needed an honest face to head the ticket; the war heroism came as a bonus. As governor, Roosevelt supported a number of reforms to improve working conditions in New York despite resistance from Republican stalwarts in the legislature. Such reformist tendencies and his resistance to party control convinced Boss Thomas Platt, head of the New York Republican machine that Roosevelt had to go. Platt had a brilliant idea. What better place to get rid of a political annoyance than in the obscurity of the vice presidency. Plat energized his minions at the party's national convention to champion Roosevelt's candidacy for the vice presidential nomination in the 1900 election. Obscurity for Theodore Roosevelt was not the result.

When he succeeded to the presidency upon the assassination of William McKinley, Roosevelt was not yet clearly identified with the Progressive movement. Nevertheless, some Republican regulars were uneasy. Presidential adviser, Mark Hanna, opposed naming Roosevelt to the national ticket as McKinley's running mate, and when Roosevelt won the nomination, Hanna presciently warned that only a bullet stood between that "cowboy" and the presidency. Roosevelt had not yet fully developed his progressive outlook, so at that time the concern of Hanna and other conservative party leaders lay more with personality and unpredictability than with policy. Roosevelt would soon give them cause for worry on all counts.

The responsibility of power worked remarkable changes in Theodore Roosevelt. A threatened coal strike as winter approached in 1902 hit Roosevelt with one of his first rude shocks in presidential politics. Expecting to chastise feisty union leaders, he invited them and representatives of the mine owners to talks at the White House. Calling such a meeting was unprecedented and signaled a new role for government. When the two sides gathered, Roosevelt was surprised to find the management representatives most unreasonable and stiffly negative, while the union men were ready to negotiate in good faith. He pressed the mine managers into an acceptable settlement and the crisis passed. Roosevelt could now look at labor and management from a new perspective.

In that same year he stunned the business community when he ordered the prosecution of the railroad trust operated by Northern Securities Company. Until then the Sherman Anti-Trust Act of 1890, weakened by debilitating court decisions, was used more often to break up labor strikes rather than for attacking corporate trusts. The Northern Securities prosecution was particularly shocking because Roosevelt took on not only one of the most powerful trusts in the country, but one controlled by three of the most powerful names in railroads and finance, E. H. Harriman, James J. Hill, and J. P. Morgan. His suit inaugurated a program of antitrust prosecutions that earned him his reputation as a trustbuster and confirmed and enlarged the misgivings of conservative party leaders.

For the rest of his term in office, Roosevelt's policies aligned more and more directly with the agenda of the Progressive movement. For years court decisions had insulated corporations from public oversight especially by the states. Now the Congress, dominated by conservatives, set up yet another line of defense. The powerful speaker of the House, Joseph Cannon; Senator Nelson Aldrich, virtual "boss" of the national Republican Party; and Senator Henry Cabot Lodge, despite his close personal friendship with Roosevelt, led the resistance to reform in Congress. Aldrich was a supreme protectionist and consistent spokesman for big business. He headed what was known as the "Big Four." He and conservative Senators William Allen of Iowa, Orville Platt of Connecticut, and John Spooner of Wisconsin dominated much of the Senate's action during Roosevelt's presidency in order to block, delay, or water down legislative efforts at business regulation. Despite their efforts, Theodore Roosevelt initiated important changes in the nature of the presidency, the American government, and the relationship of both to big business. With cunning and vigor, he pushed forward a program of reform and business regulation that included the Elkins Anti-Rebate Act and the Hepburn Act for railroad regulation, pure food and drug laws, and a massive program of conservation that withdrew millions of acres of federal lands from profitable exploitation and ecological damage by private corporations. Congressional conservatives rigidly opposed but could not effectively block these initiatives.

With instinctive governing skill, clever maneuvers, and help from Progressives of both parties, Roosevelt outplayed the conservative obstructionists in Congress. He made the presidency a more active instrument for change and invested the federal government with significant powers of oversight and regulation. The precedents he set were extremely important. This was just the beginning of an effective challenge of the U.S. government to the power of modern industrial and finance capitalism. More would come. Conservatives were distressed and distress turned to rage during the 1912 presidential campaign.

On winning election in his own right in 1904, Roosevelt made a public pledge not to run for what would have amounted to a third term in 1908, an impulsive decision he soon regretted. After he returned from his long African safari adventure in June 1910, Roosevelt expressed increasingly sharp criticism of the performance of his old friend and handpicked successor, William Howard Taft. He had expected Taft to continue the progressive thrust of his administration, but now he thought the president had fallen into the hands of the old-guard conservatives of the party. Itching to return to power and with persistent encouragement from supporters, Roosevelt decided to challenge Taft for the Republican nomination in 1912. Theodore Roosevelt won a series of state primary victories and believed that a free and fair convention would nominate him. But when Taft managers controlled the seating of delegates and convention rules, they deflected Roosevelt's challenge, and the president was renominated. Friends of Roosevelt like Elihu Root, who had served both as his secretary of war and secretary of state, and Henry Cabot Lodge, perhaps his closest friend in the political world, joined in blocking his nomination. Always a party loyalist in the past despite his policy dissents, Roosevelt now cried foul and claimed the party establishment had stolen the nomination. Within days he and his liberal supporters hastily organized the "Bull Moose" Progressive Party to challenge Taft and Democrat Woodrow Wilson for the presidency. The one-time conservative who once dismissed liberal reformers as "do-gooders" now fully identified with and even went beyond the Progressive program. His "New Nationalism" campaign pointed to a new role for the federal government. His platform called for more presidential primaries, popular election of senators, women's suffrage, more extended conservation measures, strong federal antitrust prosecutions, business regulation, minimum wage laws, an eight-hour workday, the prohibition of child labor, workmen's compensation laws, old-age pensions, and, alas, a program of national health insurance. Some of this was borrowed from the old Populist program, and much of it forecast the future New Deal of his distant cousin. His bolt from the party and this platform convinced many of Roosevelt's old conservative friends he was now a dangerous radical.

Roosevelt campaigned with all his old vigor, but with conservatives faithfully loyal to Taft, he could not overcome the effects of a divided party, and, leading the more progressive Democrats, Woodrow Wilson was elected president.

Wilson came late to political office after a distinguished academic career as a university professor and president of Princeton University. His first run for political office was his successful campaign for the governorship of New Jersey in 1910. Like Roosevelt, Woodrow Wilson was not a liberal early in his career, holding conservative economic views and expressing concern over the demands of organized labor during his years in the academic world. An alliance with the New Jersey Progressive Movement against entrenched machine corruption fed by powerful business interests converted Wilson to liberal reform ideas. His success as a reform governor vaulted him into contention for the presidential nomination in 1912. As president he pushed a progressive agenda and overcame earlier scruples about a strong federal government. President Wilson extended the program of reform begun by Roosevelt with an impressive list of legislative achievements. His first term produced a reform of the banking system with the creation of the Federal Reserve System; he signed the Clayton Anti-Trust Act with stronger teeth than the old Sherman Act, and he established the Federal Trade Commission to prevent unfair competition and abusive business practices. Wilson also supported the adoption of the Sixteenth Amendment authorizing the enactment of an income tax, to the extreme distress of conservatives then and now. Overcoming some initial reluctance, he convinced himself to support a voting rights amendment for women. During his administration, Wilson prosecuted more trusts than had Roosevelt and actively supported the full progressive program.

Theodore Roosevelt and Woodrow Wilson began the adjustment of the American democracy to the realities of modern capitalism. They broke conservative logjams, and they set important precedents for expanding the power of government, but more needed to be done. Franklin Roosevelt completed the work they began, but the opportunity for his New Deal came only after the disaster of economic collapse. These three reforming presidents fought against the brutal changes that the new capitalism had inflicted on American society. They insisted on establishing basic economic justice while preserving and defending the capitalist system from radical alternatives. At its core theirs was a conservative objective: to better sustain both capitalism and democracy. Yet their programs were uniformly, consistently, and avidly opposed by conservatives wedded to absolute capitalist freedom and unconcerned about the appeal of radical solutions, left and right, to the disillusioned and desperate. Police power, they assumed, could deal with radicals.

The trajectory from absolute free enterprise to a measure of business regulation was interrupted by international conflict. The onset of World War I distracted from the Progressive cause, and by the end of Wilson's second term, the country had apparently tired of this era of reform. Wilson suffered incapacitating strokes in the fall of 1919, and he could offer little leadership in the last year of his presidency. Conservative Republicans swept the elections of 1920, and the new decade belonged to big business and its conservative allies. The ironic result was economic disaster for the country and for the business community itself.

One of the unintended consequences of Theodore Roosevelt's bolt from the Republican Party in 1912 was the nearly complete destruction of bipartisanship in progressive politics. By 1916 Roosevelt returned to the Republican fold, but, because the party was firmly in the control of its conservative elements, many of his supports were unwelcome when they tried to return, and many others chose not to return. Liberals, as progressive politicians were increasingly labeled, gravitated to the Democratic Party, while conservative interests dictated Republican policies and candidates. The identification of the Democrats as liberal and the Republicans as conservative, always with notable exceptions, intensified through the rest of the century. By the decade of the 1920s there were only a handful of liberal Republicans, like Robert La Follette of Wisconsin and George Norris of Nebraska, still clinging to the Republican label at the national level.

Warren G. Harding, Calvin Coolidge, and Hebert Hoover, all with solid conservative credentials, steered the three administrations that dominated the politics of the 1920s. Republican majorities also controlled both houses of Congress. For the time being, Progressivism was dead. Big business and its increasingly numerous and influential lobbying associations prepared their wish lists and won everything they demanded. Federal oversight of business practices relaxed and major national scandals like Teapot Dome soon followed. In that scandal, once again corruption reached presidential cabinet level, when Secretary of the Interior Albert B. Fall was convicted of accepting oil company bribes. However, most of the benefits to capital came, not from corrupt practices, common though they were, but from friendly legislation. Business wanted tougher policies against labor and the three administrations were uniformly unfriendly to organized labor. In fact union membership declined sharply during the decade, wages remained low, and the spread between the incomes of the working class and the business class became indefensibly wide. A sharp farm recession set in at the start of the decade, but legislation to assist farmers and boost farm prices was deemed federally intrusive. When a reluctant Congress finally passed a bill to aid farmers, the measure met presidential veto. American farms failed by the tens of thousands, and the family farm faced the threat of extinction. To reduce foreign competition Congress lifted protective tariff rates to the highest levels in American history. That bit of business wisdom set off retaliatory measures by trading partners. The immediate result was a sharp shrinkage of American exports. Dangerous speculation in the stock market, even by banks using the money of unwary depositors, generated little government interest and no action. This economic program of the business establishment won unrestrained and unquestioning conservative support. During the 1920s the Gilded Age marriage of capitalism and conservatism in America enjoyed a second honeymoon.

As a consequence of this thoughtless pandering to the self-interested desires of the business community, in 1929 the American economy collapsed into the Great Depression. The United States had become the great economic power of the world. The massive increase of plant capacity during the war, a large and willing labor force, and myriad technical innovations created a giant catalog of consumer goods and invested the American economy with tremendous potential for growth. Then the economic genius of the business community set to work. Having left low-wage industrial workers and hard-pressed farmers without the resources to buy basic consumer goods, and having rigged tariff policy to assure that what could not be sold at home would not be sold abroad, American business lobbies strangled a marvelously productive consumer economy leaving it with everything necessary for success, except consumers. Neither Adam Smith nor classical conservatives could have endorsed a collection of policy choices designed to funnel a hugely disproportionate percentage of the wealth of the nation to the top 1 percent of the population. But the reigning conservative thought of that day was undeterred by history, logic, or evidence. When the stock market crashed in October 1929, a variety of excuses was offered for the "temporary" difficulties of market, and President Hoover reassured the country that the nation's economy was basically sound. Certainly, panicky government action was not necessary.

A similarly disproportionate shoveling of money to the wealthy in our own day is a matter of some interest. The supply-side fraud sold to Americans by Reaganites was supposed to lift all boats. Lower taxes on the rich, it was promised, would stimulate investment, spur economic activity, and benefit everybody. Repeated lowering of taxes on the wealthy from Reagan to the second President Bush did not produce the advertised results, but they generously benefited the already wealthy and grossly distorted the gap in net worth between the top 1 percent of Americans and the rest. This imaginative economic theory ignored the obvious. The rich, already endowed with more money than they have time to spend, tend to hoard. Tax breaks and higher wages for those of modest or low incomes will almost immediately be spent to satisfy needs and wants. That spending would, in turn, quickly stimulate economic growth. This was a lesson imprinted on the American memory by the Great Depression that followed the income distortions of the business-dominated 1920s. But the memory faded, and conservatives reinvented the discredited policy wrapped in the language of magical economic theory.

President Hoover's reassurances even as the economic crisis unfolded derived from his long held conservative social and economic philosophy. (See Appendix B.) In 1920 he published an essay entitled "American Individualism," in which he insisted that a healthy society could not survive without the motive force of individual self-interest operating in "the free running mills of competition." After maintaining order and protecting individualism, there was little need for government action in a democracy. Government activism, especially in business affairs, was inimical to the individual and to society. Hoover tied these ideas to a political philosophy he called "Americanism," associating laissez-faire capitalist ideals with the very nature of American democracy. Many conservatives soon proclaimed anyone opposed to this connection of democracy and laissez-faire economics to be "un-American." A great deal of mischief followed from this line of reasoning and the careless use of the label. These ideas held firm with Hoover for the rest of his political career, but they served him badly in the painful early years of the Depression.

Despite deepening economic decline, Hoover insisted that the nation's economic health would return and that its fundamentals were sound. He counted on the business community to lead the country to recovery and prosperity. He finally took exception to his deep convictions in 1932 by supporting the creation of the Reconstruction Finance Corporation designed to feed government money to banks and large corporations hoping for economic stimulus. By that time, the effort was too little, too late and offered little to an increasingly desperate nation with an unemployment rate heading for 25 percent. The shanty towns jerry-build from scrap metal and packing crates that appeared on the edges of American cities were derisively dubbed "Hoovervilles." Herbert Hoover's policies did not cause the Great Depression: that was the work of his predecessors. But his rigid governing and economic philosophy, elevated to the level of inviolable principle, made his response disastrously weak. Nevertheless, Hoover remained a model of righteousness and sound government for conservatives.

Franklin D. Roosevelt's New Deal powered revolutionary changes in American life and ranks in importance with the work of Washington and Lincoln. His was a revolution that grew not by chance through a pragmatic political response to the crisis of the Great Depression, but rather it rose from his long-standing and well-developed political ideology and his imbedded religious convictions.

The eighteenth-century Enlightenment phrase, adopted but not fulfilled by the French Revolution, was "Liberty, Equality, and Fraternity." All three have been part of the American democratic experience. Washington's revolution focused on liberty for Americans establishing and guiding the start of the democratic experiment that shocked and changed the world. Lincoln's revolution set the course toward genuine equality with emancipation as only the start of a long struggle for civil rights and equality. Franklin Roosevelt's revolution emphasized as never before the importance of fraternity to the health of the democracy. He brought to life the idea that Americans working in a common effort could provide for the general welfare with greater justice and security. This was revolutionary work with truly conservative consequences.

The original American Revolution led by George Washington introduced a genuine democracy to the world for the first time and created a new nation dedicated to the ideals of liberty, equality, and fraternity. Skeptical European ruling classes laughed at the Americans, and they also worried. They laughed because they thought the Americans foolish: that peasants (they were called farmers in America) should vote and hold office was simply not reasonable to the eighteenth-century European mind. They worried because they thought the American experiment might spread to their aristocratic shores. The three revolutionary ideals were not fully achieved immediately; the struggle was long and at times discouraging, but the ideals of the original revolution were indelibly set as the goals of the American democratic experiment. The stunning irony of that experiment was the persistence of the institution of human slavery. This was a contradiction that could not endure. The revolution for equality demanded an end to slavery and the recognition of the fundamental dignity of every human being. That was the work of Abraham Lincoln. Lincoln's great Emancipation Proclamation inaugurated the march not only toward freedom but also toward the ideal of full equality for all citizens. Immediately after the Civil War the first civil rights act in American history in 1866 declared equality of citizenship. The Civil War constitutional amendments also promised equality, but it took a hundred-year struggle to meet that commitment, and more is needed to perfect it.

The third revolution led by Franklin Roosevelt can be linked with those of Washington and Lincoln because of the profound changes it worked in the lives of so many Americans. It aimed to fulfill the third ideal of the original revolution—fraternity. The Roosevelt revolution elevated a proletariat into a middle class and recalibrated the material standards by which Americans could hope to live.

American historical experience from frontier days on had always combined individual effort with neighborly cooperation for the common good. Neighbor helping neighbor was vital for survival on the frontier and in the agrarian culture that followed. In a highly advanced urban and industrial society, one-on-one assistance was still helpful but inadequate. Communal help required the agency of effective government.

That working people could feed their families, live in decent housing, relieve labor with leisure, afford higher education for their children, and rest secure in old age were the conscious goals of the New Deal revolution. Roosevelt achieved them all. FDR understood that the survival of a healthy democracy demanded social and economic justice. This was especially so in a twentieth-century world of rising fascism and communism. Many Americans in the apparent hopelessness of the Depression were inclined to despair about the survival of capitalism and democracy. FDR's revolution saved both, but American conservatives never understood and never forgave.

Beyond national economic survival from the disastrous crash and Depression, which alone would have marked his administration a success, Roosevelt's vision looked beyond immediate economic recovery. He set his sights on permanent structural changes in the relationship of Americans to the economic system and to each other. In a democracy, prudence and justice demand that economic power strong enough to imperil the whole society must be subject to public scrutiny and regulation. Roosevelt understood that in an increasingly impersonal and materialist industrial economy, poverty and insecurity could endanger the very survival of a democratic society and its economic system. These ideas informed much of the New Deal.

The litany of letter agencies produced during the first weeks of Roosevelt's administration and after was designed to check the uncontrolled power of capital in the public interest. This was a perilous time that, without clear precedents or guides, called for experimentation. In 1933, during the famous "first hundred days," a nervous Congress quickly responded to Roosevelt's leadership and approved an emergency bank holiday, new banking rules, federal deposit insurance, the National Recovery Administration (NRA), the Tennessee Valley Authority (TVA), the Civilian Conservation Corps (CCC), and more. Some initiatives, like NRA, faltered; most succeeded, and the worst effects of the Depression slowly eased. In what historians call the Second New Deal, Roosevelt aimed for more permanent security and freedom from want with the passage of a minimum wage law, unemployment compensation, and, of course, the social security provisions for orphaned youth, the disabled, and the aged. Later the G. I. Bill of Rights offered government support for education and training that redirected the lives of millions. These very practical measures reflected Roosevelt's political philosophy, which was, according to his own testimony, based on his religious roots, the progressivism he embraced as a young man, and an instinctive conserving impulse. He said he was a liberal in order to be a conservative, and he saw his progressive policies in that context. One must, he said, reform if one would preserve.[2]

One is drawn to consider the importance of the Roosevelt revolution, in part, by the attempts to dismantle it. We understand a good deal about FDR and his work by the enemies he made. Even from a long distance, the visceral intensity of those who opposed him startles. An extreme and impassioned conservatism generated real hatred for the man. Hard times, we know, feed demagogues, but apart from the extremists like racist Gerald L. K. Smith and eccentric radio priest Father Charles Coughlin, bitter opposition to FDR also came from the full spectrum of conservative politics in the 1930s. The president himself believed that much of the resentment and bitterness of those who opposed him came because his work challenged the positions of privilege that had so long been held by American elites without serious challenge.

The rage of the business classes at Roosevelt bordered on incoherence. Some could not refer to him by his name but only as "that man."[3] He was called a traitor to his class. Epithets like socialist, communist, and un-American spewed maliciously from men who knew better. Once a muckraker and Progressive Movement sympathizer, Mark Sullivan was so distressed by Roosevelt's work he compared the New Deal to the actions of the Nazis in Germany.[4] Publisher David Lawrence saw the New Deal as representative of Fascist and Communist dictatorships.[5] In 1934 conservative Senator Daniel O. Hastings spoke of a Republican creed that condemned all forms of social legislation tending toward communism and called for a restoration "of liberty to the American people with only such restrictions upon it as a safe and sound social order might require."[6] When an angry Al Smith, once a Roosevelt ally now turned bitter enemy, spoke to the Liberty League, a collection of conservative business leaders, he sputtered venomously, "There can be one flag, the Stars and Stripes or the red flag of the Godless union of the Soviet. There can be only one Capital, Washington or Moscow."[7] During the presidential campaign of 1936, Herbert Hoover attacked the New Deal for trampling on the Constitution and for tax policy aimed at defeating free men and free enterprise. A "Conservative Manifesto" echoed the idea that the New Deal had attacked free enterprise, added a call for lower taxes and a balanced budget, and warned against the government's encroachment on private enterprise. One historian calls the manifesto a kind of founding charter of modern American conservatism.[8] The Republican Party platform drawn at the 1936 convention echoed these conservative convictions. (See Appendix C.) The call for lower taxes rose to the level of the highest priority on the post–New Deal conservative agenda, and there it remains. Conservative rhetoric justified lower taxes as part of the trickle-down theory that the wealth of the rich should remain untouched by government so that some of the fruit of their productive investment might seep down to the masses. The idea persists even in the face of repeated failure.

It seems clear that what began in the Gilded Age was confirmed in the 1920s and 1930s: the thoroughgoing identification of American conservatism with laissez-faire capitalism. The business ethos welded to the structure of conservative thought the idea that an unfettered capitalism was indispensable to the survival of democracy. Conservative leaders slandered liberals, accusing them of abandoning important moral and cultural values necessary for a healthy, free society. But conservative elites seemed unable to recognize the damage done to traditional values and morals by an uncontrolled capitalism. Conservatives invested the idea of the freest enterprise with the force of theological dogma with little apparent concern for its intensely materialist implications. This kind of thinking Franklin Roosevelt

challenged and discarded, insisting on reasoned restraint of the capitalist tendency to excess, and thereby he served the interests of all the
nation. After Roosevelt, from the days of what Harry Truman called
the "good-for-nothing" Eightieth Congress to the recent Tea Party
mania, conservatives have tried to chip away and reverse New Deal
reforms that challenged the materialist and amoral capitalist power
structure. According to any honest reading of traditional conservative
theory, that is a confused conservatism at work.

From yet another perspective the hostility to Roosevelt and his New
Deal programs placed a great strain on rational thought and historical
evidence. Free-market partisans, not to say extremists, ignored the
reality that American capitalism prospered mightily from Roosevelt's
legacy. In the years from the 1930s to the 1970s, an era of extensive
federal regulation of business enterprise, expansive economic and
social safety nets, and tax levies sufficient to pay for them, American
capitalism enjoyed fabulous growth in productivity, innovation, and
profits. All boats, those of lower, middle, and upper classes, rose with
the tide. Through it all the big business propaganda machine remained
hostile and feared for the survival of freedom. For conservatives to
suggest that American capitalism suffered from FDR's New Deal regulations and social programs is to be blind to logic and history.

Franklin Roosevelt and his New Deal revolution in some way
became victims of their own success. Roosevelt lifted millions into
the middle class; he opened opportunities for the working class, and
especially the uncounted number of the children of the working class,
to live well and to prosper. He created an era in which the standard of
living of virtually all Americans rose. Benefiting from his legacy, a new
generation of Americans lost touch with or never learned the history
of what, beside their own effort or good luck, made their material success possible. For many, the attraction to conservative political philosophy tended to grow stronger in direct proportion to the growth
of their income. Many of the Americans who prospered most from
the fruits of the New Deal now live comfortably with their historical
amnesia and embrace an economic and political outlook that is essentially a Social Darwinism differently dressed, but no less cruel.

Since the late 1960s American politics has experienced something of
a drought in truly progressive legislation with a growing but erroneous assumption that government is a problem and not a solution.
With his conversion to conservative enthusiasms, Ronald Reagan
broadcast with great effect the antigovernment slogans that Barry

Goldwater made popular among conservatives. That rhetoric supported a turn in American politics that smothered reform instincts, blocked necessary progressive legislation, and greatly strengthened the exploitative influence of big business in American life. Reagan and his conservative allies proclaimed a political philosophy with very unconservative consequences. To see government itself as a problem is a dangerous idea in a democracy.

Modern Conservatism: Types, Tensions, and Confusions

Though conservative opposition to New Deal reforms from the 1930s on was intense, it failed to generate broad public appeal until after 1970. Some Republicans, like Nelson Rockefeller of New York and Henry Cabot Lodge Jr. of Massachusetts, tried to put some distance between themselves and Roosevelt-hating conservatives by modeling themselves as "Modern Republicans." That group persuaded retired general Dwight Eisenhower, the war hero of no discernable political record, to run for president as a Republican in 1952. The party followed their lead in rejecting the staunchly conservative Robert A. Taft for the nomination, choosing Eisenhower instead. President Eisenhower's was not a liberal administration, but he did not try to turn back New Deal reforms. In fact, the president cooperated with liberals in extending Social Security coverage to more than 10 million people. He also expanded unemployment insurance benefits and supported raising the minimum wage from 75 cents to $1. Despite Ike's moderate policies in tune with liberal precedents, his was also a very business-friendly administration including a cabinet stocked with corporate lawyers and executives from big business. Nevertheless, Eisenhower's refusal to turn back the New Deal was a matter of some distress for conservatives like Senator Barry Goldwater of Arizona and William F. Buckley Jr., founder of the new voice of conservatism in America, the *National Review*. Both men stirred new excitement in conservative circles in the 1950s. A fierce anticommunism marked the era. Conservatives were impassioned in their rants about the dangers of the "evil empire," a term of later coinage, though anticommunism was embraced across the political spectrum during the decades of the Cold War. The Truman administration originated the NATO defense alliance, the Kennedy administration reacted fiercely to communism in Cuba, and Lyndon Johnson justified the enlargement of American involvement in Vietnam as a necessary step to halt the advance of communism in Asia. In the summer of 1964, the Tonkin Gulf resolution that gave Johnson a virtual blank check for military action in Vietnam passed the Senate with opposition from only two maverick skeptics. Wayne Morse of Oregon and Ernest Gruening of Alaska were both regarded as somewhat eccentric, though they turned out to be prophetic on that issue. Although anticommunist fervor was not exclusive to conservatives, slanders like "twenty years of treason" hurled at the administrations of Roosevelt and Truman did not encourage bipartisanship. Senator Joseph McCarthy of Wisconsin was particularly adept at painting liberals as "pink" or worse. Goldwater and Buckley were only a little more subtle, but no less suspicious. They linked their anticommunism to a defense of capitalist freedom, and their support for uncontrolled free enterprise was complete and unremitting.

Conservatives howled at the expansion of progressive domestic programs of the Kennedy-Johnson era. Determined to resist, a revived conservative movement again hissed at big government and chanted incessantly in favor of liberating free enterprise from regulatory restraints. Not all conservatives, however, applauded that objective. A certain brand of conservatives had never reconciled to the changes wrought by the explosion of industrial and finance capitalism. Those classic conservatives could not abandon the older traditions for surrender to the materialist ethic of modern capitalism. But those who clung to genuine conservative thought had long ago retreated into an almost complete silence or remained fellow travelers in the capitalist-subservient modern conservative movement. Some still persist in this confusing alliance. A sympathetic observer wondered why the modern American conservative remained "so blind to the tremendous power that some private men wield over other private men as to insist the only real danger to liberty in industrial society is 'government ascendency'?"[1]

Worries about the cultural and moral consequences of free-market capitalism persisted among a coterie of traditional conservatives for many years. Recall the hostility of the Adams brothers, Henry and Brooks, to a burgeoning finance capitalism. As conservative political operatives tied themselves more and more closely to an unqualified defense of free-wheeling capitalism, those conservatives who identified with long-standing, traditional conservative values grew increasingly uneasy. At times during the twentieth century some important conservative thinkers of traditional disposition wrote of their concerns. Unfortunately, they were largely ineffective within the modern conservative movement, and, sadly, some of them softened their critique of capitalism and joined in conservative efforts to turn the word "liberal" into a pejorative label.

Surviving traditional conservatives were a varied collection. A brief survey will illustrate.

In 1930 a group of 12 Southern intellectuals, often called the Southern Agrarians, published the book *I'll Take My Stand* in defense of the Southern agrarian tradition. They defended the "humanism" of traditional Southern culture and railed against the materialism and commercialism of mass industrial society, which they saw as dangerous to ethics and morals. They emphasized the importance of rural life, tradition, family, religion, local communities, and the need to defend spiritual values against the materialist pressures for mindless consumption. *I'll Take My Stand* regretted the passing of an agrarian world and the new dominance of an industrial, technological world. This heartfelt lament protested the inevitable. The discoveries of science and technology that stimulated industrial productivity and growth could not have lain fallow in order to preserve a simpler agrarian social and political structure that, however benign in memory, did not alleviate the periodic economic misery of the mass of people. The fabulous productivity and the unforeseen social changes that capitalism stimulated were the irrepressible products of human ingenuity, inventiveness, ambition, and greed. That the new capitalism should dominate society without oversight or restraint was another matter.

The Southerners assessed the character of modern capitalism from a conservative perspective and found it unpalatable. The authors bemoaned its influence on the decline of family relations, and one contributor, Lyle Lanier, accused modern industrialism of fostering patterns of conduct "incompatible with the conditions necessary to the stability and integrity of family life."[2] In the introduction to the manifesto, the authors called on Southerners to resist the encroachments of this new capitalist regime. From a distance of over 80 years, *I'll Take My Stand* is still highly regarded as an eloquent statement of conservative values. Others read the book as a somewhat sentimentalized and romanticized view of the old South and a sad and somewhat naive call for history to stop. But it is, nevertheless, instructive and adds to the evidence of classic conservative doubts, indeed, profound fears, about the impact of capitalism on conservative values.

Conservative scholar Richard M. Weaver knew the work of the agrarians; he was a student of John Crowe Ransom at Vanderbilt University and a colleague of Robert Penn Warren at Louisiana State University, two of the authors of *I'll Take My Stand*. In *Ideas Have Consequences* in 1948, Weaver offered arguments against laissez-faire and deplored the materialism of free competitive capitalism as degrading to human beings. Defenders of private property, he insisted, should "oppose much that is done in the name of free enterprise, for corporate organization and monopoly are the very means whereby property is casting aside its privacy." With some irony he noted how business groups were seldom shy about seeking help from government.[3] Weaver lamented the impact of free-wheeling capitalism on the culture, but his book was short on proffered solutions. He did once offer a truly odd suggestion given his defense of traditional social and moral values. In an essay on conservatism and libertarianism he wrote, "I therefore can see nothing to keep him [the conservative] from joining hands with the libertarian, who arrives at the same position by a different route, perhaps, but out of the same impulse to condemn arbitrary power."[4] But there was no power in the land more arbitrary than the power of unelected big capital. Weaver's proposal was doubly odd given the intensely unconservative social and political agenda of libertarians. Weaver stands as a good example of a classic conservative who expressed his fears about the effects of capitalism, but failed to break with those modern conservatives who identified capitalism with Americanism and unrestrained economic freedom.

More recently, another conservative voice spoke to the problem of modern conservatism in its relation to free-enterprise capitalism. Former Marxist-turned-Christian conservative, historian Eugene Genovese, was also a great admirer of the best of Southern culture and tradition. In 1994 he wrote sympathetically about the ideas laid out by the authors of *I'll Take My Stand* and of their conservative, precapitalist agrarian sympathies. He noted that Southerners of classic conservative leanings recognized that capitalism dissolves "traditional social relations." This is true of capitalist enterprise generally, but Genovese described the multinational corporations that dominate world finance and production as the worst culprits. He condemned them as "literally irresponsible. They operate under few if any moral restraints." Nightmarish fears about the free market dogged Genovese. In a powerful passage, he confessed his fear of a future dominated by an "international economy of morally indifferent affluence for many and misery for those who cannot compete."[5] It seems that his old sympathies for the working class did not entirely evaporate after his new embrace of conservatism.

The work of the often-controversial conservative Peter Viereck was suspect in some conservative circles with good reason. Viereck lamented how conservatism in America had "degenerated into a facade for either plutocratic profiteering or fascist style thought-control nationalism." He was critical of Buckley's *National Review* for its devotion to free-market economics and its support for the candidacy of Barry Goldwater. He applauded the Southern agrarian attack on commercialism and condemned the decline of twentieth-century conservatism by abandoning its Burkean roots in favor of laissez-faire economic individualism.[6]

Roger Scruton, an English philosopher, is much admired in conservative circles for his book *The Meaning of Conservatism*. In struggling to define conservatism, Scruton mused about the ties of modern conservatism to a free-market economy calling it "simple minded." Such an economy inevitably resulted in monopoly of business oligarchy, limited genuine competition, and developed power to challenge the state. He rejected the notion that government regulation of enterprise is an evil undermining of individual rights. Another conservative English philosopher, Michael Oakeshott, expressed similar thoughts insisting that unregulated competition was a "chimera" and regulation by law did not necessarily destroy competition and, indeed, might be necessary to preserve it.[7]

These were minority views among conservatives, but they came from the most highly respected conservative intellectuals and represented an important line of thought among conservative theorists who regarded themselves as classic or Burkean conservatives. No Social Darwinism stained their writing. They could not reconcile market-driven, unregulated capitalism with a conservative program in defense of traditional values in a humane society. How then could modern conservatives organize enthusiastic, unquestioning, and passionate energy on behalf of the demands of capital and resist virtually any government efforts to moderate the most pernicious effects of the free market?

One of the most highly respected conservative thinkers of the twentieth century was Russell Kirk. He, too, was a conservative in the tradition of Edmund Burke, whom he much admired, especially for Burke's openness to reform and his genius in being able "to discern the difference between a profound, slow, natural alteration and some infatuation of the hour." This skill seemed to be lost in the passions of the new conservatism. He defined a statesman in Burkean terms as "one who combines a disposition to preserve with an ability to reform." Another of his heroes was Benjamin Disraeli, whom he counted as a conservative capable of humane change. Here was a conservative who worked for the passage of the British Reform Act of 1867, enlarging the franchise, and who supported Factory Acts, aid to education and the beginnings of public housing. Disraeli aimed to draw the growing British working classes to the ultimately conservative Tory causes of crown, church, and order. There was also something of Hamilton in Kirk's thought that "Leadership by men of ability, birth, and wealth is one of the most material, and most beneficial aspects of civilized life."[8] In a new edition of his classic work, *The Conservative Mind* (1986), this eloquent spokesman for traditional conservatism laid out six cannons of conservative thought. As a statement of the conservative mind, they are worth citing in precise detail.

1. "Belief in a transcendent order, or body of natural law, which rules society as well as conscience. Political problems, at bottom, are religious and moral problems."
2. "Affection for the proliferating variety and mystery of human existence, as opposed to the narrowing uniformity, egalitarianism, and utilitarian aims of most radical systems."
3. "Conviction that civilized society requires order and classes against the notion of a 'classless society.' "
4. "Persuasion that freedom and property are closely linked."
5. "Custom, convention, and old prescriptions are checks both upon man's anarchic impulse and upon the innovator's lust for power."
6. "Recognition that change may not be salutary reform: hasty innovation may be a devouring conflagration, rather than a torch of progress."[9]

The Russell Kirk Center, dedicated to carrying on his legacy, now publishes a document on its website titled "Ten Conservative Principles," adapting a statement from Kirk's book *The Politics of Prudence*, published by his estate. Here Kirk expanded the 6 listed above to 10 and repeated the same essential conservative message, but the two lists have a particular omission in common. In neither list is there any suggestion of a paean to free enterprise or a rant against government. Kirk rejected individualism if it meant social atomism, and he insisted on the importance of community. Considering this collection of ideas, it is difficult to explain Russell Kirk's long association with Barry Goldwater and the conservatives around William F. Buckley Jr. He supported Goldwater in his presidential campaign in 1964, and he wrote for the *National Review* for many years despite growing increasingly distressed by the ideas on government and economics the Buckley establishment trumpeted. It is also odd that in what is probably his most important work, *The Conservative Mind*, a book of some 500 pages, Kirk said little about the perversions of conservative thought by figures like the extremely libertarian Herbert Spencer and William Graham Sumner, and little about the challenge that a very materialist capitalism poses for genuine conservatism.

His most recent biographer quotes Kirk's argument that economic liberalism "laid the foundations of the technological order in the new industrial society of the nineteenth century." The result was a decay of community standards, morals, and the family.[10] Here Kirk is using the nineteenth-century meaning of "liberal" economics, that is, the economics of unregulated free enterprise. So the real indictment in his remarks is not of twentieth-century liberal regulatory and social reforms, but it is precisely a condemnation of the corrupting effects of laissez-faire capitalism. This analysis by Kirk adds to the puzzle of why he could so closely associate himself with that kind of capitalism so dear to the Buckley, Goldwater, and Reagan conservatives of the last half of the twentieth century. His biographer remarks, "The parallels between the emergence of Russell Kirk as the great intellect behind conservatism and Barry Goldwater as the national spokesman of the conservative movement are striking."[11] Why this was so in view of Goldwater's support for intensely laissez-faire economics, his admiration of Ayn Rand, and his libertarian views on abortion and other moral and social issues of the day defies explanation of any clarity.

There are more puzzles about Kirk's conservatism. He detested the utilitarianism of Jeremy Bentham for its materialism and its welded identification of the good with the useful, with all the moral pitfalls that implied. He also repudiated the libertarianism of Ludwig von Mises (see below), which he deemed tied to Bentham's "liberalism." He also challenged libertarian economist Friedrich von Hayek in debate, attacking Hayek's insistence that truly free enterprise was the path to genuine progress. On this subject he wrote, "Behind Hayek's chain of reasoning seemed to lie the assumption that if only a perfectly free market economy could be established, all social problems would solve themselves in short order."[12] Kirk rejected Hayek's vision, but not the similar views of the beneficence of the free market held by his friends in the American political arena like Goldwater and Reagan. Even as he praised them, he reflected on the condition of the United States and said, "Our obsession with fast cars and our longing for the prestige of a suburban house have driven freeways remorselessly through a thousand living communities, destroying everything in their path."[13] The regret he expresses here is in fact a curse on the consumerist, materialist culture of laissez-faire capitalism.

Kirk admired the papal encyclicals *Rerum Novarum* of Leo XIII and *Quadragesimo Anno* of Pius XI. Both were sharply critical of laissez-faire capitalism, its concentration of wealth in the hands of the few, and its abuses of the working masses. One would search in vain for such thoughts in the pages of the *National Review*.

Kirk once implied that conservatism and liberalism were different but not polar opposites. "The process of growth involves the process of reform." The key is identifying the difference "between necessary and desirable alteration, and unnecessary and undesirable destruction." Tradition should be the guide for such judgment according to Kirk. He cautioned that devotion to tradition should not be allowed to "sink into mere unquestioning routine." A balanced and reasoned respect for tradition is compatible with support for necessary change. How should tradition guide? It should teach that important discoverable truth lies in tradition and that family and church are transmitters of tradition. Tradition suggests the humanization of urban life and the preservation of small town and rural communities. Traditional truths illuminate conditions of the present. Kirk rued the fact that modern life, having lost a sense of continuity with tradition, was "drenched in propaganda, aimless amusement, and the flood of sensual triviality." But neither in this exhortation and critique nor elsewhere does Kirk recognize the ties of a decline of traditional values and the vulgarization of culture to the materialist driven, libertarian capitalism so avidly supported by modern conservative movements. Rather he simply blamed liberals and radicals for failing "to show us any road to the redemption of mankind from modern boredom and modern decadence."[14] One is moved to wonder whether he really expected movements on the left to assume the functions and responsibilities of religion, a highly unlikely and profoundly unwelcome prospect for both religion and liberalism. One must also ask if the redemption of mankind is really to come from the free market.

Kirk's caution against hasty change might be taken as a warning to liberals inclined to easy change, but it should also be noted that there are no forces more stimulating of thoughtless and irrational change than market forces that drive capitalist enterprise to ever greater profit. Religious and ethical consideration may influence individual entrepreneurs, but there is no moral prescription in the economic theories that underpin laissez-faire free enterprise. Capitalism is not necessarily immoral in its operations, but it is amoral and culturally indifferent. The essential purpose of capitalist enterprise is to produce a profit. The sleazy pit of vulgarity into which the mainstream media has descended, posing bad taste as entertainment for the sake of selling hamburgers, antacids, or tampons, has cheapened modern popular culture. Illustrating even more acutely the moral indifference of capital enterprise is the production and distribution of pornography, currently a significant and immensely profitable investment to which one can subscribe through legitimate stock market purchases. These are mere examples that could be multiplied many times, but conservative objections to the cheapening of the culture are rare or barely whispered. When objections are raised by writers like Kirk, they are largely ignored and have little effect on the politics of conservatism. Think of the near-obscenities of the incessant advertising that jams the media. Think of a clothing industry that turns styles appropriate to streetwalkers into high fashion and does not shrink from pushing the suggestive in clothing for the preadolescent. Think of the promotion of consumerism, planned obsolescence, and waste that coarsens and pollutes the culture. These are graphic illustrations of the distance between traditional Burkean conservatism and the blind association of conservatives with unqualified support for laissez-faire capitalism that has contributed generously to rapid and thoughtless cultural changes hardly in tune with traditional conservative ideals.

Gary Wills was once a close friend and ally of William F. Buckley and frequent contributor to the *National Review* until divergent views led to a somewhat bitter break. Wills came to read capitalism as an instrument not for conservation but for change. "If it is strange to see capitalism posing as individualist, it is even odder for it to act as the voice of conservatism." "There is nothing less conservative than capitalism. ... [I]t razes to rebuild; it destroys to employ."[15]

Irving Kristol, once a strong liberal voice who became a fervent convert to the conservative faith, grew to question some of its verities. For him the iron association of capitalism and freedom was at least exaggerated in view of the history of governments that combined economic freedom with political and social repression. Meditating on the unqualified conservative embrace of modern capitalism left him uneasy. Capitalist economic theory offered nothing to restrain investment in those vehicles of press and media that corrupted traditional moral values. There had been a shift in the United States, he argued, "From having been a *capitalist, republican community,* with shared values" to a *"free, democratic society* where the will to success and privilege was severed from its moral moorings." Kristol's friend, sociologist Daniel Bell, agreed that twentieth-century capitalism in America was possessed of no moral ethic, was a principal agent in the distortion of old small town life, and had embraced a hedonist materialism. Free enterprise, he feared, had become economic oligopoly "destructive of social needs."[16]

Conservative pundit and columnist George Will confessed similar concern about the corruption of Burkean conservatism when he complained that American conservatives should be embarrassed to invoke Burke if they also believe, as many do, that "conservatism is capitalism, no more no less." Will feared that Americans were reducing conservatism to an economic doctrine. With a keen eye for irony, he also noted that Karl Marx was right in claiming that capitalism would undermine traditional moral structures. Will worried that capitalist influence cultivated the growth of a culture favoring instant gratification. He saw Milton Friedman's laissez-faire faith as essentially libertarian and incompatible with conservatism. Libertarianism encouraged the "dissolution of public authority and other restraints needed to prevent license from replacing durable, disciplined liberty."[17] None of this, however, restrained Will from encouraging and cheering for the victory of libertarian, antigovernment, economic conservatives at the polls.

The misgivings noted were not attacks on laissez-faire capitalism by liberals or radicals; these were the voices of tradition-minded conservatives pointing to the dangers capitalism presented to conservative values. Why they remained allied to modern, laissez-faire conservative political campaigns in consistent alliance with libertarian groups remains unexplained. An important leader of the libertarian right, Grover Norquist bristled at the less-libertarian social conservatives like Kristol and Will, who, while often critical of government, did not see government as truly evil. And yet in the end, Kristol and Will remained boosters of the modern conservative movement that welcomed libertarians to its cause, apparently not unduly concerned about the problems with libertarianism over which they fretted.

Clearly there was a divide between these traditional conservative thinkers and the ideas that dominated American conservatism since its Gilded Age capture by corporate capitalism. While the traditionalist worried about the direction of modern conservatism, their resistance to the trend was neither vigorous nor noticeably effective. Conservatism since the mid-twentieth century revived late nineteenth-century enthusiasms and rededicated itself to the service of capital and to a passionate economic individualism.

~~~

There is seldom unanimity in ideological creeds of the right or the left. For example, the variety of Marxist sects since Marx and Engels published their *Manifesto* challenges the cataloger. So, too, the conservative brand of politics has displayed a great range of opinion. There were key differences among individuals and clearly identifiable divisions in the conservative movement during the second half of the last century. However sharp the differences, the varieties of conservative thought all clung to the idea that government regulation of capitalist excesses constituted a major threat to freedom.

William F. Buckley Jr. and his allies shaped one branch of modern conservatism. It is not a gross exaggeration to credit Buckley and his host of friends whose work appeared in his *National Review* with a revival of interest in and commitment to conservatism in American politics beginning with their critique of the Eisenhower presidency. Buckley launched a crusade in defense of free-market economics and conservative stands on social issues. Ayn Rand inspired a different version of conservative thought with a set of ideas she called Objectivism. Rand championed a revival of Social Darwinism without apology, and she drew a large, enthusiastic, and influential following. Rand thought the idea of the common good and the proposition that a nation should tend to its social obligations were fictions created by the weak to undermine the strong. Her conservatism was purely libertarian and Buckley hated it. The partisans of these two approaches to conservatism clashed, sometimes bitterly, but on one principal tenet there was general agreement: a belief in antigovernment, laissez-faire capitalism, without which freedom could not survive. There was sufficient common ground under this doctrine to clear the path to active cooperation and partnership in the political arena as Richard Weaver foresaw.

The differences were not trivial. Buckley and company wanted to dismantle much of the structure of government especially as it touched economics and social welfare, but they believed there was an important role for government in maintaining law and order, fighting foreign dangers with a particular obsession about communism, and even a role for government in sustaining traditional moral and cultural values including action against what was traditionally regarded as immoral behavior. The disciples of Ayn Rand were and remained libertarians who also hated communism, but they saw little for government to do beyond national security, traffic control, and preventing crime, narrowly defined. Promoting traditional moral or cultural values was not on the libertarian program of government functions. Buckley rejected Rand's atheism, while she remarked that Buckley was too intelligent to believe in God. Buckley drew on his interpretation of Christianity to see conservatism engaged in a mortal struggle with atheism; Rand was a propagandist for atheism who hated religion in general and Christianity in particular. Despite Rand's antireligious apology for capitalism, some Republican leaders still invoke her work, and her books remain popular with conservatively inclined readers of fiction. Her novels still sell in the thousands of copies every year. They entertain, but hardly serve as examples of high literature. The more likely reasons for continuing sales are the libertarian ideology embedded in the stories and the fact that conservative groups distribute copies as propaganda vehicles. Despite the not insignificant differences in the two conservative outlooks, the adherents of both versions climbed into bed together, and they railed against even the most modest liberal proposals. Both offered unqualified support for the demands of free-enterprise capitalism.

The group of writers and political operatives Buckley assembled as a vanguard of the new conservative thrust could hardly be described as classically conservative. There were clearly unbridgeable tensions between the free-market conservatives and the conservative theorist like Kirk and Weaver. The first issue of the *National Review* listed the principles to which the journal would be committed. These proclaimed that government should be limited to the protection of life, liberty, and property, because other activities of government would only diminish freedom and hinder progress. Despite its editorial rejection of libertarian philosophy, Buckley's *National Review* consistently promoted intensive free-market positions embracing the libertarian economic formulas of Friedrich von Hayek, Ludwig von Mises, and Milton Friedman. Buckley deemed free economic competition necessary for liberty and progress, and he believed the nation should defend an organic moral order. His journal often argued the importance of religion in society and defended right-to-life stands (but not a total ban on abortions). Its view of government and competition won libertarian applause; to followers of Rand, the call for a defense of natural law and upright morals did not appeal.[18]

Buckley's commitment to free-market ideas was so absolute that it powered his dissent on a point of church teaching despite his firmly held Roman Catholic religious commitment. As strong as his faith was, he could not accept the developing papal perspectives on social and economic justice. In 1961 Pope John XXIII issued his encyclical *Mater et Magistra*, an updating of Catholic teaching on economic justice since *Rerum Novarum* of Leo XIII and *Quadragesimo Anno* of Pius XI. The new encyclical challenged free-market ideas that left capitalists to their own devices. Among other reservations about capitalist behavior, John cautioned that wages should not be determined purely by the laws of the market that fell short of justice and equity. He regretted the contrast between the persistent extreme poverty in the world and the wealth and luxurious life of the few. Going beyond the earlier documents, Pope John stood open to the idea that the state should intervene in the economy when the economic power of private individuals could injure the community at large. The encyclical looked to "systems of social insurance and social security [that] can contribute to the redistribution of national income according to standards of justice and equity." These were hardly radical ideas, coming from one of the most consistently conservative institutions in the Western world. The *National Review* editorialized that the encyclical was a "venture in triviality." Buckley published his personal response to the encyclical saying, "Mater, si, Magistra, no" (Mother, Yes, Teacher, No), generating a combination of distress and derision in some Catholic circles.[19]

Part of Buckley's strategy for a resurgent conservatism directed an appeal to youth. He was instrumental in the founding of Young Americans for Freedom in 1960. His thought is evident in the group's inaugural proclamation, the Sharon Statement, so called because it was drafted at Buckley's home in Sharon, Connecticut. Much of the draft was the work of M. Stanton Evans, who became associate editor of the *National Review* in 1960 and remained in that post until 1973. Buckley's perspective comes through clearly. The young people announced in Stanton's voice that they believed

> That liberty is indivisible, and that political freedom cannot long exist without economic freedom;
>
> That the purpose of government is to protect those freedoms through the preservation of internal order, the provision of national defense, and the administration of justice;
>
> That when government ventures beyond these rightful functions, it accumulates power, which tends to diminish order and liberty;
>
> That the market economy, allocating resources by the free play of supply and demand, is the single economic system compatible with the requirements of personal freedom and constitutional government, and that it is at the same time the most productive supplier of human needs;
>
> That when government interferes with the work of the market economy, it tends to reduce the moral and physical strength of the nation; that when it takes from one man to bestow on another, it diminishes the incentive of the first, the integrity of the second, and the moral autonomy of both.

It should be noted that Buckley and his supporters, young and old, insisted that the free-enterprise market economy was not only the best or the preferred system, but the *single* economic system compatible with individual freedom and constitutional government. Absolutism in defense of economic freedom was deemed no vice. Especially impressive is the assertion in the last paragraph that interference with the market generated *moral* decay. Buckley's supercilious disdain for the efforts to establish social and economic justice in the work of FDR, Harry Truman, John Kennedy, and Lyndon Johnson's Great Society programs was constant, but he had little alternative to offer except the mystic cure-all of unrestricted capitalism and private goodwill.

For all of his commitment to capitalist enterprise, Buckley was no sycophant to American businessmen and could unleash his occasional testiness on them. He once described the American capitalist as "the inarticulate, self-conscious, bumbling mechanic of the private sector" "fleeing to the protective arms of government at the least hint of commercial difficulty, delighting secretly in the convenient power of labor unions to negotiate for an entire industry." He acknowledged that businessmen loved Ayn Rand's novels, but with characteristic cutting wit he concluded, "it transpires even as Russell Kirk predicted, that her novels were read not because of their jackbooted individualism, but because of the fornicating bits."[20] Buckley offered unqualified admiration for the capitalist system, but not for its practitioners, and his skillful pen could slash at both his allies in the business community and his libertarian competitor in the struggle for the hearts and minds of conservatives.

Ayn Rand fled Soviet Russia for the United States in 1926. She was among the first women allowed to earn a university degree in Russia, but she despised the Communist regime. She held in common with the regime only her atheism, which she embraced at an early age. After earning her university degree, she studied cinema arts in Russia, escaped to America, and made her way to Hollywood, finding work in production and writing in the movie world. Fame came with the publication of her novel *The Fountainhead* in 1943 and more broadly with *Atlas Shrugged* in 1957. In these works lay the bases for the collection of ideas she labeled and broadcast as Objectivism. In line with her atheism, its elements included the emphatic rejection of religion and any belief in the supernatural, which she regarded as superstitious and harmful to human progress. Taking a cue from Friedrich Nietzsche, whom she greatly admired, she rejected Christian morality as destructive to the human person, especially because it called for assistance to the poor and put the common good ahead of the self. She emphasized the power of human reason, which she thought was confined to and dependent completely on sense data. For Rand the only reality was material reality. Much of this thinking she shared with run-of-the-mill Marxists, but her hatred of Marxism came through clearly. Marxists proposed a communal response to a purely material world; Rand moved in the diametrically opposite direction to a thoroughgoing individualism. Individual self-interest based on what she called ethical egoism should govern human behavior. Each person should live only for his own sake, without sacrificing for others or seeking sacrifice from others. She disdained altruism, proclaimed selfishness a virtue, and insisted that the uncompromising pursuit of self-interest was the path to individual happiness and social progress.[21]

Applied to politics Rand's ideas translated into a complete commitment to minimalist government and to the freest laissez-faire capitalism as the only acceptable economic system for individual and social progress. Capitalism was a social system as well as an economic system and required an absolute right to private property for proper function. All property should be privately owned. Although she rejected political anarchism and had arcane reservations about being associated with the label "libertarian," her work was, in fact, an important influence on the growth of libertarian political sentiment within

American conservatism. She and her disciples joined in conservative political causes, but from the beginning tension and even hostility developed between them and conservatives like Buckley, who remained committed to and driven by religious beliefs. For example, Whittaker Chambers, a close associate of Buckley and frequent contributor to the *National Review*, wrote a review of *Atlas Shrugged*, panning it for making individualism an end in itself and for its atheism and materialism. Alan Greenspan, one of Rand's friends and fervent supporters and later chairman of the Federal Reserve Board, complained to Buckley that Chambers was a man "beneath contempt" for his comments on what he called Rand's masterpiece.[22]

Rand was not the only source from which the libertarian streak in American conservatism drew. Robert Nozick, a professor of philosophy at Harvard, inspired conservatives of that ilk. In *Anarchy, State, and Utopia*, Nozick posited the benefits of the minimal state. Government should be confined to "the narrow functions of protection against force, theft, fraud, enforcement of contracts." Beyond such functions, action by the government could only violate individual freedom. The state should certainly not use its power to compel individuals to contribute toward aiding others.[23]

Also widely respected in conservative circles, Frank S. Meyer rejected the humane concessions to the role of government in the thought of conservatives like Russell Kirk and Peter Viereck, whom he referred to as pretentious for offering "another guise for the collectivist spirit of the age." He called for a reconciliation of the difficult combination of tradition and libertarianism in the postwar conservative movement. He urged commitment to a belief in an objective moral order together with an emphasis on individual liberty against the collective and a free economic system. But he differed from pure libertarians when he cautioned against individualism unguided by objective moral values.[24]

Both branches of postwar American conservatism inspired by Buckley and Rand called on the work of academic economists to support their attacks on government and their defense of unrestrained capital. Some economists mounted a challenge to the work of John Maynard Keynes, who had inspired the New Dealers and whose work was widely accepted by most mainstream economists. Keynesian economics prescribed a strong role for government in avoiding recession or inflation by managing interest rates and in stimulating or restraining economic activity through tax policy and public spending. Keynes argued that when a recession threatened, the government should lower interest rates and taxes, and increase spending even if it resulted in an unbalanced budget. This was not only permitted; it was essential to stimulate growth in the economy. In an economic boom if inflation threatened, then that was the time to increase interest rates, increase taxes, lower spending, and balance the budget. Franklin Roosevelt, though reluctant, adopted Keynesian policies to fight the Depression with good results. All such was anathema to conservatives, who saw Keynesianism as the beginning of a slide to inevitable collectivism. A small number of academic economists spoke their language and shared their prejudices. Buckley and his friends frequently cited three important economists even though they also fed the libertarian tendencies in American conservatism.

Milton Friedman of the University of Chicago was a special favorite of conservatives for his attacks on government spending and regulation, his support for lower taxes, and his insistence on the beneficence of the free market. A prolific writer and Nobel Prize winner in economics, Friedman was highly respected for his technical work in the field even by economists who did not share his politics. There was a gap between his technical contributions to economics for which he won broad praise and his economic politics less widely applauded. He insisted with more faith than science that a free market was essential for personal freedom. With strong libertarian inclinations, Friedman repeatedly proposed that most government functions be privatized and that the graduated income tax, minimum wage laws, and even Social Security pensions be abolished. He concluded his 1962 best-selling apologia for unchained enterprise, *Capitalism and Freedom*, with an ominous warning that big government concentrates too much power in the hands of elected political authorities. He ignored, however, the danger to freedom from the concentration of power in the hands of big capital, whose managers are responsible to no electorate. Against big government a democratic polity can at least vote the current crop of rascals out of office. Against the perfidies of the mega-capitalists there is little recourse.

Friedman sealed an iron-clad connection of freedom to free markets and swore a total commitment to libertarianism. "Underlying most arguments against the free market is a lack of belief in freedom itself." "Few trends could so thoroughly undermine the very foundation of our free society as the acceptance by corporate officials of a social responsibility other than to make as much money for their stockholders as possible." These views informed his advocacy of privatizing virtually all government functions outside the realm of maintaining law and order. For Friedman, culture and morals were matters of individual concern with no connection to public policy.[25]

Friedman admired the work of another academic hero of conservatives, Austrian-born, British economist Friedrich Hayek, who also taught at the University of Chicago. He, too, contributed to what became a conservative postulate by insisting that democracy was possible only in a capitalist society. In 1944 he published his most famous work, *The Road to Serfdom*. Any significant limit to free enterprise paved a road directly to socialism, and therein lay peonage. Government involvement in economic matters was death to freedom and inevitably led to totalitarianism. Proposals for income redistribution or measures to insure basic social justice were mischievous, unnecessary, and dangerous. A little less draconian than Friedman, Hayek allowed that some rights to property must be limited so its use did not damage others or the society, and he saw some benefit in ideas like a minimum wage. But competition was essential to freedom and required a legal system designed to preserve it. The president of the Sun Oil Company, J. Howard Pew, who had inherited the business from his father, was so taken with Hayek's ideas that he wanted to send copies of *Road to Serfdom* to ministers across the country. He was a devout Presbyterian and recognized in Hayek's book an opportunity to convince people of the link between religion and capitalism. He could not have fully understood the libertarian implication of Hayek's thought. Hayek distanced himself from traditional conservative concern for stable culture and good order. In an essay, "Why I Am Not a Conservative," he argued that conservatives of classic beliefs do not sufficiently support liberty. They admire authority and this interferes with liberty.[26] To embrace Hayek's ideas was to reject a principal tenet of classical conservatism.

A third scholar buttressing the libertarian side of conservatism was Ludwig von Mises, like Hayek, a member of the Austrian school of conservative economists. He rejected government planning as totally incompatible with capitalism; indeed, he regarded "planning" as a code word for socialism, communism, and authoritarianism. "There is no other planning for freedom and general welfare than to let the market system work." His libertarianism was without limit. The only legitimate function of a government was to provide its people with security against attacks by criminals and defense against foreign enemies. "We see that as soon as we surrender the principle that the state should not interfere in any questions touching on the individual's mode of life, we end by regulating and restricting the latter down to the smallest detail." Personal freedom is then lost.[27] Neither Hayek not Friedman liked the label "conservative"; they preferred to be described as classical liberals in the nineteenth-century context, which implied support of free enterprise. They cheered the American conservative adoption of free-market fundamentalism as a kind of political religion, a faith that also demanded the denigration of government. With cultural conservatism they had no sympathy.

A few conservatives like Irving Kristol lamented the lack of any conservative cultural agenda in the ideas of Friedman, Hayek, or Von Mises. Kristol worried that none of them saw any need for restraints "on the libertine tendencies of modern bourgeois society." The tendency of libertarian capitalism to cut free from traditional moral restraints, he thought, constituted a kind of pernicious nihilism. The capitalist is willing to produce and sell culturally debasing material including pornography and call it "just another splendid business opportunity."[28]

As is true of liberals, there was clearly a wide range of particular differences and emphases among individual conservatives. Those who called themselves conservatives, however, might be grouped into three somewhat distinctive categories. A significant number of traditional, Burkean conservatives survived who emphasized the importance of cultural conservatism without insisting that uncontrolled capitalism is absolutely essential to sustain a free society. Their principal concerns lay with a well-ordered society able to balance individual freedom with community responsibility. They sought to sustain religious institutions and values, and they lamented the materialism and relativism that so deeply infected modern life. In an ideal world such conservatives would be capable of cooperating with liberals on many issues while offering some healthy tempering restraint of liberal enthusiasms. In the American conservative world, that cooperation was not possible, nor were they measurably effective in moderating the extremes of materialist and individualist tendencies of conservative politics.

Diametrically different were the libertarians; they called themselves conservatives but saw little value in tradition or religion. For them society was best served by an individualism marked by intense self-interest and government of minimal responsibility. A third conservative constituency one might associate with the followers of Buckley and their many sympathizers who marched in the revival of postwar conservatism. With limited success Buckley and company tried to reconcile with elements of the other two conservative types despite their incompatibility. These hybridizers were as stubbornly defensive of laissez-faire economics as the libertarians, even while pressing conservatives to uphold traditional and cultural values. They tended to glide over the inevitable tensions between traditionalists and libertarians, and they were especially blind to the antitraditional, materialist, and morally indifferent character of modern capitalism. In the end traditional conservatives like Weaver and Kirk were relegated to the background. Such men could neither become apostate, joining with liberals, nor could they be comfortable apologists for the free market. But both remained supportive of a distorted American conservative political movement.

From the 1970s forward, supplementary interpretations of what was essential to conservatism added more complexity and some additional confusion in defining modern conservatism, but they had no visible effect on loosening the grip of capitalism on the direction of conservative action. In the last third of the twentieth century the work of televangelists and other religious groups introduced a surge of concern over issues like abortion and gay rights that drove many of what are called social conservatives into political action. They constituted yet another source of tension with libertarians who rejected legislative interference with individual moral choices or "lifestyles." Popular preachers like Jerry Falwell called for a return to traditional religious values to fight the secularism of the day, but he and other preachers also seemed to baptize capitalism. Falwell was an enthusiastic supporter of Ronald Reagan for president. He founded a group called the Moral Majority to support conservative stands on social issues and conservative candidates for public office. Falwell saw biblical sanctions for laissez-faire capitalism. Leading a good conservative Christian life, the message went, would be rewarded by God with material blessings. Falwell and others like him preached a modern version of the nineteenth-century Gospel of Wealth. The connection between conservatism and capitalism remained undisturbed, indeed, frequently endorsed by much of the fundamentalist religious establishment. The preaching tended to equate Christianity and capitalism and even revived the Gilded Age notion that material success was a sign of God's favor.[29]

Adding still more to the complexity of conservative thought was another political phenomenon of the last decades of the century: the rise of neoconservatism. This was not an organized movement. The term refers to a group of intellectuals, initially drawn initially from New York Jewish political thinkers whose careers as political activists and commentators had been distinctly liberal, even radical in some cases. They were led by men like Norman Podhoretz, editor of the journal *Commentary,* and Irving Kristol, editor of *Public Interest.* Both journals were converted from advocacy of liberal reform to vehicles in support of conservative causes and Republican candidates. Podhoretz and Kristol were joined by other former liberals like Michael Novak, Ben Wattenberg, Midge Decter, Jeane Kirkpatrick, and William Bennett, among others. Though resisting the label "neo-conservative," liberals like Patrick Moynihan and Daniel Bell were sympathetic to some neoconservative interpretations of American domestic policies. In foreign policy, the core neocons argued for an aggressive posture toward the USSR, while it still existed, and some of their heirs were very vocal and influential advocates of American

Middle East interventionism including the Iraq and Afghanistan Wars, from whose unintended consequences the world still suffers.

The neoconservatives reacted, some would say overreacted, to the extreme postures of the "new left" radicalism of the 1960s. Most liberals of the FDR, Harry Truman, John Kennedy stripe, like Hubert Humphrey, Robert Kennedy, historian Arthur Schlesinger, and economist John Kenneth Galbraith also rejected new left extremism. Those new left enthusiasms soon dissipated, especially after U.S. withdrawal from Vietnam, but neoconservative fears only grew more intense. They discovered a new kinship with the American conservative movement in a near-panicky fear of the Soviets and in domestic economic and social issues. They saw the United States in a condition of moral and cultural crisis, and they were dismayed by the impact of the social chaos of the late 1960s. Neocons believed, with much exaggeration and little credit for the real reduction of poverty, that Lyndon Johnson's Great Society programs were wasteful failures. Meanwhile they developed a new appreciation for the fruits of capitalist enterprise. They praised the obvious productivity of American capitalism, which, they proposed with some novel reasoning and scant evidence, could provide the real answer to eliminating poverty. They embraced the notion of long standing in conservative circles that capitalism and democracy were necessary for each other. To reach this conclusion they glided smoothly past the historical reality that capitalism and authoritarian governments had often coexisted quite compatibly (Hitler's Germany and Mussolini's Italy were notable examples) and that democracy survived in good health in countries of mixed and highly regulated economies.

Among the most widely read and effective spokesmen of neoconservatism was Irving Kristol, sometimes called the godfather of the movement. In books and in contributions to a variety of publications including op-ed columns in the *Wall Street Journal,* he sang the praises of laissez-faire capitalism and repeatedly identified capitalism with human freedom, despite some significant reservations noted above. Kristol even bought into the illusions of "supply side" economics touted as a panacea during the Reagan years, and he supported the full economic agenda of Republican conservatives. He also joined their calls for tax cuts for the investing classes and endorsed the idea that a government active in the economy was a danger to all.

Despite the generous applause for capitalism and its multiple benefits to society, neoconservatives harbored some serious concerns about the system and the antics of some of its more avid champions. This was especially true of Kristol, one of whose books he titled *Two Cheers for Capitalism.* Though his neoconservative conversion drove him to support laissez-faire economics, Kristol recognized some of the crudities of the system and could not completely abandon his pre-conversion commitment to social welfare. Despite the newly discovered respect for the efficiencies and the political and economic benefits of free-market mechanisms, he explained that neoconservatives were "not libertarian in the sense, say, that Milton Friedman and Friedrich A. Von Hayek are. A conservative welfare state . . . is perfectly consistent with the neoconservative prospect." His earlier reservations persisted and intensified. Writing in the conservative magazine *The Weekly Standard*, as late as August 2003, Kristol cited an American culture in decline, reaching "new levels of vulgarity." In this view he tied neocons to traditional conservatives, but not to libertarians "unmindful of the culture." A decent society requires restraints and ought to respect the religious and cultural traditions from which those restraints are drawn. To this end the libertarian streak in capitalist-driven culture fails.

Kristol echoed these ideas in the op-ed columns he wrote for the *Wall Street Journal*. These were often critical of the questionable ethics and the profligacy of American capitalists. He continued to associate capitalism and human freedom, but he feared that capitalism had succumbed to libertarian temptations and was left without a moral compass. Important segments of the business community accepted neoconservative support, but ignored their ethical recommendations.[30]

With fewer reservations and even more explicit in the association of capitalism and freedom was the neocon Michael Novak, who became an important figure in the American Enterprise Institute, a think tank devoted to the defense of capitalism unchained. By 1970, having abandoned his liberal convictions, Novak warned that capitalism was vulnerable and under attack. In one of his projects at the American Enterprise Institute he wrote, "democracy apart from capitalism is very difficult to achieve. Between capitalism and democracy there is an underlying system of mutual reinforcement and internal harmony." A devout Catholic, he also crafted a Christian theology of capitalism, weaving together thoughts about God, democracy, and free-market capitalism. Among the truly startling revelations in that odd gospel was the idea that the corporation was "a much despised incarnation of God's presence in this world." To serious students of religion this was a stunningly new perspective on pantheism. Despite his faithful commitment to the Catholic Church, Novak also expressed serious reservations about those papal encyclicals that assailed the materialism and greed so often reflected in capitalist enterprise. The popes apparently misunderstood the theological implications of the capitalist system.[31]

As a group neoconservatives were selective in their muffled criticism of capitalist behavior. They had little to say about the multibillion-dollar cost to Americans from the savings and loan catastrophe foisted on the country in the 1990s. The repeal of regulations limiting the risks the savings and loan financiers could take with their depositors' money was almost immediately followed by high-risk speculation and inevitable collapse. Nor was there significant criticism of the stimulus failures and giant debt magnification that resulted from supply-side Reaganomics. A distinct neoconservative identity has faded some, but neither the survivors nor their heirs have had much to say about the thievery that produced the collapse of Enron in 2001. Nor have conservatives of any stripe had much that is believable to say about the connection between the repeal of New Deal banking regulations and banking scandals of 2008 and the great recession that resulted.

The tensions cited within neoconservatism mirrored the problems within the American conservative movement at large. Conservatism was and remains pulled in different directions by its libertarian wing, its traditionalists, and its big-money financial engines in support of the freest capitalism. In this mix, despite the tensions, the capitalist agenda has thrived: markets freed of regulation and restraint, lower taxes for the wealthy, and less government because "government is the problem." These are accompanied by much posturing and noise making on social issues of conservative concern but little effective action. Opposition to abortion, resistance to gay rights, concern about illegal aliens, and immigration policy draw many to the conservative label, but capitalist economic interests still dominate American conservative politics. Despite the concerns of rank-and-file conservatives especially in the southwest, it is no oddity that closing borders to a potential low-wage workforce generates little enthusiasm in big business circles or the conservative think tanks they finance.

Since the last decades of the twentieth century, conservative efforts in defense of capitalism have been benefited by the massive contributions of capitalists to political campaigns of trustworthy candidates. Through a kind of political money-laundering process employing political action committees and "think tanks," corporate money financed thinly veiled propaganda engines in support of free enterprise. In his *Wall Street Journal* columns, Kristol urged businessmen to fund research in support of the business agenda. Some had anticipated the call; others, wakened to the possibilities, were happy to comply. The rosters of the boards of directors of these organizations read like a who's who of American big business. One of the earliest of them was the American Enterprise Institute founded by a group of businessmen in 1943. More recent and very influential organizations include the Heritage Foundation (1973) and the Cato Institute (1977). By 1980 the American Enterprise Institute enjoyed the support of over 600 contributors from among American corporations. The stated aim of the American Enterprise Institute was "to defend the principles and improve the institutions of American freedom and democratic capitalism." The Cato Institute intended to defend the free market, lower taxes, and cast doubt on the efficacy of the welfare state.[32]

The president of the Cato Institute, John A. Allison IV, published a book in 2013 that denied that the manipulations of giant financial institutions were responsible for the great recession that followed the banking debacle of 2008. The book clearly captured the tenor of the institute's libertarian ideology. Allison confined the role of government simply to protection against foreign tyrants and to the prevention of fraud and the illegitimate use of force. Beyond these basic duties the actions of government only redistribute income from the productive to the unproductive and destroy innovation and creativity. The subtitle of his book is "Why Pure Capitalism Is the World Economy's Only Hope."[33]

The Cato Institute, the American Enterprise Institute, and similar organizations have worked consistently to identify freedom with free-market capitalism. Their biggest contributors included beer magnate Joseph Coors; Richard Mellon Scaife, heir to the Mellon banking fortune; and passionate libertarians David and Charles Koch. The Coors family has been especially generous in funding conservative think tanks. The Coors have been described as supporting "a return to Darwinian political and economic morality formed by the unrestricted demands or market and capital." The Coors Corporation provided a quarter million dollars to fund the first year's budget for the Heritage Foundation in 1973. It is not surprising that these organizations repeatedly published papers in support of lower taxes and deregulation of business enterprise. These big-money agents virtually constituted an arm of the Republican Party producing propaganda supportive of the aims of the corporate world. One result was a marked intolerance for any dissent in conservative circles on issues concerning taxes and government spending. One searches in vain for this kind hostility to taxes and government action in the writings of traditional conservatives in the past.[34]

Political action committees also served business-friendly political causes and raised money for political candidates by reaching beyond the legal limits of individual contributions. By the mid-1980s business-oriented political action committees outnumbered those funded by prolabor groups by 1,700 to 400. Organizing for assaults on government regulation, corporations expanded their hiring of lobbyists to prowl the corridors of government in numbers that went from about 175 Washington lobbyists in 1971 to almost 2,500 in 1982.[35] Such were the tools and defined goals of American conservatism by the end of the twentieth century. Burkean conservatives blushed, but remained muted if not silent.

American conservatism since the end of World War II has been a mix of diverse and sometimes contradictory political sentiments. The single most consistent feature dominating the movement has been the largely uncritical support for a new Darwinian capitalism that overwhelmed and submerged traditional and revered conservative principles. That unblushing embrace of libertine capitalism molded the character of American conservatism. While social and moral issues concerned many conservatives, the libertarian influence in the movement dominated conservative political action in legislatures, state and national. Great disdain for government, focus on unrestrained individualism, hostility to the idea that the economically less fortunate are deserving of any public aid, and unquestioning support for business platforms from opposition to a decent minimum wage to fervent support for thoroughgoing deregulation have all won conservative applause. As these libertarian impulses prevailed, conservatives seemed to revive all the doctrines of Social Darwinism without the evolutionary trappings, and they called it the American way. Those opposed, therefore, were "un-American" and somehow unpatriotic. Samuel Johnson was not far wrong when he described perverted patriotism as "the last refuge of scoundrels." Once capitalists adapted conservative ideas to the impassioned service of free enterprise, the genuine conservative faith suffered from divisive and heretical tensions. Their insistent identification with laissez-faire enterprise, libertarian individualism, and materialism pushed aside and inevitably eclipsed concerns for tradition, stability, organic change, and civic virtue. A few conservatives saw the contradictions and offered somewhat mild criticism. Most remained silent witnesses. Capitalist enthusiasts embraced the whole package, contradiction and all. One historian of right-wing politics suggested that real conservatism was abandoned in the nineteenth century. The triumph of industrialism "generated an all-pervading climate of materialism that made it possible for men to identify capitalism and democracy."[36] That conservative doctrine and conservative political action should be placed so unreservedly at the service of capital would have caused Edmund Burke to blush with embarrassment.

6

The Politics of Conservatism

The postwar surge of political action by American conservatives began in earnest with the Barry Goldwater presidential campaign of 1964. Goldwater, a Republican from Arizona, was elected to the Senate in 1952. He rose to prominence in Arizona politics supporting the buildup of industries moving to the Sunbelt by arguing for tax breaks, government subsidies, and restrictions on union organizing. Goldwater dedicated himself to making his state a free enterprise oasis, but without objections to government subsidies. He launched his political career as a business-friendly, union-hostile conservative. With more imagination than common sense, he once described Walter Reuther, president of the United Auto Workers Union, as more dangerous to the United States than "anything Soviet Russia might do."[1] The business community supported his political ambitions with enthusiasm. He soon became a favorite of conservatives who were receptive to his criticism of the Eisenhower administration as too moderate and too reluctant to reverse the liberal policies of the past. As noted, Eisenhower was persuaded to run for president by the moderate wing of the Republican Party, and he agreed with them that the nation should accept the permanence of the New Deal social and economic reforms. He recognized that persistent economic inequality could be a great danger to the country. Many businessmen and especially leaders of the National Association of Manufacturers were dismayed if not shocked by Eisenhower's accommodation with reality. A more extreme reaction came from a paragon of the lunatic Right, Robert Welsh, founder of the John Birch Society. He suggested Eisenhower was a Communist agent. While that was, indeed, an extreme reaction, the rising wave of conservative sentiment in the 1950s brought into play the idea that free enterprise in America was under attack, and many on the Right rejected Eisenhower's realism.

Goldwater sparked new life into the smoldering resentment against the New Deal among the business classes and focused much of his political rhetoric on the charge that the government itself was the enemy of prosperity and progress and a danger to American freedom. It took some time for the message to sink in, but with years of repetition the conservative mantra that government was the problem had its impact on public opinion. During the early 1960s Goldwater became the premier conservative spokesman in opposition to the liberal policies of the Kennedy/Johnson administrations. Though personally friendly with John Kennedy, he was a severe and occasionally caustic critic of efforts to build on and expand New Deal liberalism. In line with most conservative sentiment of the day, he also voted with the southern bloc in Congress in resistance to civil rights proposals, which he interpreted as an aggrandizement of the power of federal government and an intrusion into the rights of the states.

Enjoying the spotlight in national political debate and perhaps with an eye on a presidential bid, in 1960 Goldwater published *The Conscience of a Conservative,* much of it written by Brent Bozell, brother-in-law of William F. Buckley Jr. A small book of less than 130 pages, this somewhat simplistic summary of conservative positions became a kind of user's manual for the conservative movement. For Goldwater, conservatism was not merely a political posture; it derived from the "truth that God had revealed about his creation" and from human nature. The positions he then laid out set the standard conservative menu for the future with unalloyed support for the alliance between conservatism and capital. In classic conservatism, government was not a target of attack in itself. But since any significant harnessing of the power of capital and meaningful regulation of business would certainly come at the hands of government, the conservative/capitalist alliance now dictated that a government strong enough to be effective was unacceptable. Goldwater and his supporters labeled such a government a danger to individual liberty and charged moderate Republicans were as guilty as Democrats for refusing to embrace the concept of limited government. That the rights of black Americans were trampled by the states and that the federal government was finally taking important steps toward protecting civil rights went unacknowledged by Goldwater and his conservative supporters. He argued that government had historically been the instrument for crushing man's liberty. Wage earners were abused and subjected to the whims of labor leaders, and encouraged by government, unions had too much power and did great damage. On the other hand, waves of unnecessary government regulation handcuffed businessmen and slowed progress. In making the point that too much legislation was mischievous, Goldwater's language tangled him in a lapse of logic. "I will *not* attempt to discover whether legislation is needed *before* I have *first* determined whether it is constitutionally permissible." The rights of the states were absolute in those areas constitutionally reserved to them, he believed, and that included questions of civil rights. He also insisted "that the Constitution does not permit any interference whatever by the federal government in the field of education." The Supreme Court decision on integration of schools was, therefore, mistaken. He labeled the graduated income tax a confiscatory tax aimed at reducing men to a common level. Reduced spending and lowering taxes would guarantee the economic strength of the nation, and Republicans, too, had been lax on these matters. Social Security payroll taxes were an unnecessary burden on both businesses and workers, and social security should be a private, not a government, concern. That privatization would cripple the social security protections of the aged and the disabled in America did not deter conservative Republicans from repeating the proposal from time to time.

Conservatives could also read with pleasure Goldwater's charge that the welfare state was an instrument of collectivization, and this "Socialism-through-Welfarism" was a danger to freedom. His allies never tired of repeating Goldwater's claim that welfare creates wards of and dependence on the state. That there were unfortunate poor was a fact, but care for the needy should not be the concern of the state and should be left to private charities. That private charities had never been able in the past and could not now possibly serve adequately the overwhelming numbers in rural and urban poverty was apparently not a matter of serious concern. The last chapter in his confession gathered the extant condemnations of communism and warnings about the Soviet menace.[2]

Goldwater identified his conservatism with a strongly libertarian economic individualism. He described the conservative movement as one "founded on the simple tenet that people have the right to live life as they please, as long as they don't hurt anyone else in the process." While he grew his program on a theist root, Goldwater spoke little of cultural and social conservative issues. He was hostile to and publically attacked the influence of the religious Right on the conservative movement, and he refused to endorse its social objectives including opposition to abortion rights. After he left the Senate, he joined the National Republican Coalition for Choice, and he openly criticized discrimination against gays.[3] The core of his conservatism lay in his unflagging support for business and his hostility to government. *The Coming Breaking Point*, a book he published in 1976, confirmed the character of his political creed. The book took a pessimistic look at the future of an America suffering from too much government.

Government regulators placed obstacles in the paths of business success by imposing too many restrictions in the name of safety and the environment. Even the most basic protections for the environment were unacceptable to Goldwater. For example, he complained at length that the government handcuffed the automobile industry by requiring the unnecessary installation of catalytic converters in cars to lessen air pollution. Conservative political resistance to cleaning the environment has a long history and matches neatly the opposition of business lobbies to environmental legislation. This should be no surprise since those lobbies have consistently funded conservative political campaigns. The book also attacked the social security system, the "excessive" influence of labor unions on government (at a time when that influence was in fact waning), and it equated business regulation with the betrayal of that vision of freedom inherited from the Founding Fathers.[4]

In the 1960s, support for Goldwater came from all sides of the conservative family. The *National Review* described *The Conscience of a Conservative* as forthright and a "pleasure to read." Ayn Rand endorsed his candidacy for president in 1964 despite his affirmation of God. While Rand's vision of a godless capitalism upset some conservatives, Goldwater admired her libertarian themes in *Atlas Shrugged*. Buckley, Kirk, and other leading conservatives lavished praise on their standard bearer. But conservative enthusiasm was not enough. Despite intense conservative support, Barry Goldwater lost his bid for the presidency to Lyndon Johnson in 1964 in a landslide. The conservative hour had not yet come. On the surface this election result could be interpreted as a rejection of conservatism and an endorsement of New Deal policies given the announced War on Poverty and other social and economic reforms Johnson inherited from Kennedy and incorporated in his Great Society vision. Not immediately obvious was the growing popularity of conservative ideas and the determination of conservatives to make a difference in the Republican Party and American politics. Better than the election results, the Republican nominating convention earlier that year had forecast the future.

The convention turned into a showdown between competing wings of the party. The modestly liberal Modern Republicans were still led by party stalwarts like Rockefeller; Lodge; William Scranton, governor of Pennsylvania; and Mark Hatfield, governor of Oregon. These men, who enjoyed the support of the now-retired Dwight Eisenhower, saw the Republican Party's future success in an accommodation with and the responsible administration of an America whose modern structure of social and economic safety nets and business regulation derived from the New Deal. They were confronted by the Goldwater wing of the party that longed to repeal that history. In the end, the Goldwater forces controlled the convention. When Rockefeller took the podium to address the convention, delegates greeted him with boos and hisses. And when his speech began with a warning about the danger of extremists to the party and the nation, the jeering became raucous and persisted until the embarrassing end of this speech. The now-dominant conservative faction of the party clearly and loudly repudiated Rockefeller and the moderates. Since then no presidential candidate has won the nomination of the Republican Party without at least the tolerance, if not the enthusiasm, of the right wing. In his acceptance speech, Goldwater shot a last jab at Rockefeller and the moderate Republicans with an exhortation that drew a long roar of approval from the delegates when he affirmed that "extremism in defense of freedom is no vice" and that "moderation in pursuit of justice is no virtue." In addition to the requisite warnings about the dangers of communism, much of the speech was devoted to a defense of private property as a bulwark of freedom and to the danger to that freedom from too much government. In now-standard conservative language, beyond national defense, the proper function of government should be limited to being fiscally responsible, encouraging a free enterprise economy, and enforcing law and order. Government paternalism was false security and a step toward abandoning freedom.

In November, the American electorate was not responsive to the conservative message, choosing Lyndon Johnson by overwhelming numbers, but new life had been breathed into the conservative movement. Although Barry Goldwater's star faded in the years that followed, the movement he inspired attracted a new army of adherents, munificent financial backing from capitalist moneyed interests, and the allegiance of a new conservative hero.

Ronald Reagan traveled a circuitous route from Hollywood to Washington and from activist liberal to conservative icon. While the journey took him to very different places, it is possible to identify a certain consistency of purpose in the itinerary. Reagan remained committed throughout to concepts of democracy, freedom, and a just society providing for the common good. For a time he understood these goals were best served by the Democratic Party. Seeking the better means to achieve and defend these ideals led him to some acute course adjustments.

Reagan began his encounter with politics as an enthusiastic supporter of Franklin Roosevelt and the New Deal and as a union representative for the Hollywood motion picture community. He joined the board of directors of the Screen Actors Guild in 1941 and eventually served as its president for seven years. During that time he was a committed Democrat who was intensely anti-Communist in a new red scare era. As was the case with other red scare claims of Communist subversion, the dangers of Communist influence in the movies were exaggerated by ambitious political opportunists. To the distress of many of his colleagues in Hollywood, Reagan cooperated with congressional investigators seeking to expose Communists sympathizers working in the motion picture industry. He remained a Democrat for a time, but an increasingly uneasy one. His association with the General Electric (GE) company as television host for the General Electric Theater produced a pivotal turn in his career and his thinking. Although still a Democrat in the 1950s, his political sympathies drifted dramatically to the right. He supported Dwight Eisenhower's presidential bids, and in 1960, though still nominally a Democrat, he endorsed Richard Nixon over John Kennedy.

As part of his duties for GE, Reagan delivered motivational speeches to business and civic groups across the country, making more than 130 appearances over a period of eight years. Filled with conservative verities, the pro-business talks revealed the depth of his ideological shift in favor of the now-standard right-wing postures: less government, freer enterprise, and lower taxes. For his new role he was advised and trained by GE vice president Lemuel Boulware. Boulware's encouragement and strategic planning pointed Reagan toward a political career. The inevitable political transition came in 1962 when Reagan formally joined the Republican Party. He endorsed and campaigned for Goldwater in 1964, and one of his campaign speeches titled "A Time for Choosing," later dubbed *The Speech*, became famous among supporters as a definition of Reagan's conservatism. He presented his audience with a challenge to choose either freedom and order or the path to totalitarianism. The speech was a partisan collection of the ideas that had been developed for his GE tours, now honed and polished for the political arena. He praised the work of private business and attacked the welfare state as creeping socialism; big government and high taxes endangered freedom. The speech carried a strongly libertarian flavor. The function of government was to maintain order; everything else should bow to individualism.[5] Reagan was a big hit on the campaign trail, and the conservative establishment eyed a new potential star with delight. His libertarian sympathies remained constant, and they blended easily with other current conservative perspectives. In an interview with the libertarian magazine *Reason* in July 1975, he said he believed that the "heart and soul" of conservatism was libertarian.

In 1965 a group of wealthy businessmen organized a Friends of Ronald Reagan Committee to promote his candidacy for governor of

California in the 1966 election. The men promoting Reagan were self-identified conservatives, but they would not have been recognizable as such by a committed Burkean conservative. Political analyst Haynes Johnson described them as latter-day Social Darwinists, "a familiar American type, self-made men who espoused rugged individualism, free (that is, unfettered and unregulated) enterprise, and a belief in the survival of the fittest." Government action was to be judged by the degree to which it interfered with their interests. One member of the committee, Justin W. Dart, was a Reagan friend of long standing. He enjoyed great wealth as a result of a long career in executive roles in Walgreen and Rexall drug companies, Avon products, and Tupperware. His Dart Industries eventually merged with Kraft foods. Dart made clear the purpose of promoting Reagan as a candidate. He dismissed the hot issues of the day like abortion and civil rights as trivial; they come and go. As far as he was concerned, the overriding issues were "our economic health, economic leadership, or economic dominance, and our military defense ability."[6]

Men from the corporate world dominated the Friends of Reagan Committee, and they eagerly poured money into the campaign. Reagan challenged incumbent Governor Pat Brown, who was running for his third term. Brown won his second term by defeating Richard Nixon in what the media mistakenly considered the end of Nixon's political career in 1962. The Reagan campaign portrayed Brown as a tax-and-spend Democrat, soft on crime, and tolerant of welfare cheats. Reagan had by then come a long way from his days as a union rep. At one point in the campaign, the *San Francisco Bee* quoted Reagan's lament that unemployment insurance provided a "pre-paid vacation for freeloaders." The campaign strategy paid off, and Reagan won a landslide victory, taking more than 57 percent of the vote. American conservatives had a new star.

Despite occasional references to God and a rhetorical commitment to conservative social issues, the decidedly libertarian streak in Reagan's conservatism came through in his actions as governor. He spoke of a return to spiritual values while he promoted an economic individualism of intensely materialist character and consequence. He appealed to social conservatives, but in 1967 he signed what was at that time the most permissive abortion law in the country. He also approved the country's most liberal divorce law in 1969, and he opposed and helped defeat a referendum proposal that would have banned homosexuals from employment in the schools. The libertarian deviations did little damage. His popularity among the nation's conservatives only grew stronger in the years that followed, and he eventually replaced Goldwater as the darling of the Right.

In 1976 Reagan challenged reigning President Gerald Ford for the presidential nomination. Ford had stumbled into the presidency when a bribery scandal forced the resignation of Spiro Agnew as vice president, and the collection of Watergate scandals drove Richard Nixon to resign as president. Those embarrassments and an intense economic problem with inflation left Ford vulnerable. Despite a rather conservative voting record during his time in Congress, which endeared him to the right wing, Ford was associated by some with the moderate wing of the Republican Party. With his challenge of Ford, Reagan's popularity among conservatives rocketed. Nevertheless, the Republicans, still traumatized by the scandals and resignations, chose not to turn away from a sitting president. Ford was nominated after a tough convention fight, but the trajectory of Reagan's career was clear to all.

His public appearances and his political action committee, Citizens for the Republic, generated continuing interest in Reagan. By 1980 he was ready for a serious run for the presidency. While pursuing the nomination and defeating Jimmy Carter in the election, Reagan ran on a solidly conservative platform that was critical of the federal government, supported states' rights, and promised lower taxes and a smaller national budget (except for the military). These goals he repeated in his inaugural address with special emphasis on the dangers of government. (See Appendix D.) Although missing from some published versions of the text, the audio recording of the speech contained one of the most often-quoted Reaganisms. "Government is not a solution to our problems; government is the problem." To the special delight of the libertarian wing, the line has continued in use as the mantra of the American conservative movement.

During his presidency, Ronald Reagan drew strong and consistent support from the conservative religious Right that had grown more powerful in its social and political influence during a new era of fundamentalist revivalism. Reagan made more frequent religious references in his public speeches, and tele-preachers like Jerry Falwell and Pat Robertson were lavish in their praise for the president as he reversed his earlier position and now condemned the *Roe v. Wade* abortion decision. Although he repeatedly endorsed the social positions struck by the evangelists, there was little in the Reagan record of legislative action in behalf of these goals.[7]

The Reagan presidency brought to fruition an important shift in American political sentiment. It converted millions to a set of ideas that defined American conservatism in ways that should have made traditional conservatives cringe. Those ideas added up to an only thinly disguised Social Darwinism whose principle impact was to drive government policy toward the service of the richest and most powerful elements of the capitalist establishment. The Reagan administration pushed a program of deregulation that rolled back or eliminated New Deal protections against the excesses of Wall Street. Republicans embraced deregulation, proffered as a stimulus to the economy, with great fervor, and many Democrats, frightened by what they perceived to be the trend of public opinion, meekly fell in line with varying degrees of reluctance in the years that followed. Many business regulations that remained on the books were rendered impotent by exquisitely relaxed enforcement by the Justice Department and agencies like the Securities and Exchange Commission. The multiple scandals of the 1980s and 1990s on Wall Street, on the Chicago Mercantile Exchange, and in the collapse of the savings and loan industry met with conservative silence. The distinction between the world of investment and a giant gambling casino dimmed more than slightly with conservative encouragement.

The management of the economy also suffered from the revival of old ideas in new packaging. In economic planning the theories of Arthur Laffer exerted a strong influence on President Reagan. A member of the president's Economic Advisory Board, Laffer promoted the benefits of what came to be called the Laffer curve. His theory held that there was an optimum rate of taxation that would produce maximum revenue for the government, and the optimum was not the highest rate. Here was an idea eminently useful to the conservative cause, because Laffer insisted that the optimum rate for the greatest return was lower than the existing tax rates, which, therefore, should be substantially cut. With calculations defying logic and experience, the theory insisted that lowering taxes would not only increase government income but also stimulate production and boost the economy by leaving more money in the hands of the well-to-do for investment. Reagan did not require a great deal of prodding to buy the theory. These ideas fit neatly into what was called supply-side economics. Increasing production and the supply of goods, Laffer assured the untutored, would eventually stimulate demand and boost economic activity. Exactly how creating a glut of goods would spark demand among consumers of limited means remained somewhat obscure. The positive results, however, were touted as a sure thing. The more money accumulated by the top earners of the society, the greater the stimulus to the economy. Some of this prosperity would eventually trickle down to those of more modest incomes and everyone would prosper. George H. W. Bush, when he challenged Reagan for the presidential nomination in 1980, referred to these theories as "voodoo economics," suggesting the formula had a mystical, magical, or phony quality about it. Though he was right, "voodoo economics" was a phrase Bush later regretted and quickly abandoned when he accepted Reagan's invitation to be his vice president.

David Stockman was another key economic adviser to Reagan. He served as the director of the Office of Management and Budget until 1985 and was, at least publicly, devoted to supply-side ideas. He led the effort to lower taxes and to shrink the monies available to fund key social programs. One result of implementing supply-side theory was that government income never rose to the predicted or desired levels, and the budget deficits and national debt grew massively during the Reagan years. For decades, conservative politicians had loved to blame the accumulated national debt on liberal spending policies. The Reagan years increased the national debt to record levels. Conservatives amnesia leaves this uncomfortable fact about President Reagan's legacy irretrievably buried. During his tenure in the administration, Stockman was a conservative favorite, but after he retired from the Office of Management and Budget, an attack of candor damaged his reputation in those quarters. An essay based on a lengthy interview with Stockman published in *Atlantic Monthly* (December 1981) contained Stockman's admission that supply-side theory was like a Trojan horse designed to reward the wealthiest supporters of the party. He and other insiders knew that program would not fulfill its promise. But it did provide a rationale for pushing tax reductions through Congress with unavoidable cuts in social programs to follow. Stockman later referred to supply-side Reaganomics as "radical, imprudent and arrogant." The theory defied the broad consensus among professional economists; it ran counter to the president's balanced budget posturing, and it was, in fact, an illusion. The inevitable budget deficits left no alternative to cutting an array of liberal domestic programs enacted in past decades. In 1985 Senator Patrick Moynihan of New York, a long-time friend of Stockman, spoke publicly about the ruse. He told the *New York Times* that Stockman had confided to him that the administration knew the supply-side tax cut would not work as advertised. The purpose was to create "a strategic deficit that would give you an argument for cutting back the [social] programs that weren't desired."[8]

Another source of conservative inspiration for Reagan and conservatives generally was the work of George Gilder. He was one of Reagan's favorite and most quoted authors. Gilder's work suited Reagan's sympathies toward business enterprise and his public deference toward religion as president. Gilder tried to establish a kind of theology of capitalism with a new Gospel of Wealth and a modified version of civic religion. There are moments when the unkind might wonder whether these thoughts emerged from some deeply religious revelation or from an equally strange, substance-induced mystical experience. While entrepreneurs were not sinless, Gilder informed the faithful, "more than any other class of men, they embody and fulfill the sweet and mysterious consolations of the Sermon on the Mount and the most farfetched affirmation of the democratic dream." The rules governing the world of enterprise, he insisted, were guided by two familiar religious exhortations: " 'Do unto others as you would have them do unto you' and 'Give and you will be given unto.' " The poor were poor not as victims of the system, but simply because they refused to work hard. He complained that professional economists (who subjected his ideas to ridicule) failed "to capture the high adventure and redemptive morality of capitalism." He was critical of cultural conservatives like Aleksandr Solzhenitsyn, Daniel Bell, and Christopher Lasch for their criticism of the materialism and moral ambiguities of capitalism. There was no selfishness in capitalists seeking tax cuts and other benefits, Laffer insisted, for these were steps toward economic boom for the whole society. This was a most convenient theology for the moneyed faithful, but it served as another betrayal of traditional conservatism.[9] It is astonishing that so many bought into a conservatism that now openly endorsed theories formulated by the well-to-do insisting that society would be best served by arranging for the wealthy to become wealthier.

Ronald Reagan's presidential labors, ostensibly aimed at reducing the size of the federal government, led instead to the reduction of the effectiveness of government's regulatory responsibilities even as the size of the government actually grew during his regime. Government oversight was frustrated not only through neglect and lax enforcement but also by outright corruption, all in the service of free enterprise. The Department of the Interior was an arm of government with particular responsibility for protecting the environment. The tenure of President Reagan's secretary of the interior, James G. Watt, is instructive.

Watt came to the administration from the Mountain States Legal Foundation, an organization he helped to establish with funds from billionaire Joseph Coors, who was also an early supporter of Reagan for governor of California. That organization was dedicated to economic liberty and limited government and lobbied hard for the reduction of environmental restraints on commercial development. Watt was unapologetically opposed to new legislation to protect the environment, slowed the enforcement of federal regulations already enacted, and relaxed restrictions on mining companies operating on federal lands. Equally indifferent to environmental concerns was his associate, Anne Buford, whom Reagan appointed to head the Environmental Protection Agency (EPA). She and her aide, Rita Lavelle, were

accused of mismanaging funds appropriated for environmental super-
fund cleanup projects, and Buford was held in contempt of Congress,
forcing her to resign. In related cases, over 20 EPA officials were also
removed from office at that time. Rita Lavelle was indicted for perjury
and sentenced to prison in 1984. Questionable ethical standards
prevailed with regrettable frequency among Reagan appointees.
Over 200 Reagan administration officials were indicted for offenses
on the job, a challenge even to the squalor of the Nixon years. These
included Michael Deaver, Reagan's deputy chief of staff convicted of
ethics violations and perjury, and Watt himself, indicted on multiple
counts of perjury and obstruction of justice. A plea bargain kept Watt
out of prison and limited his punishment to five-year's probation, a
fine, and a period of community service.

Reviewing the well-known details of Ronald Reagan's political
career exposes the thin connection of late twentieth-century conservatism to the tenets of the genuine conservative tradition. The driving
force, the actions, and the enthusiasms of Reagan-inspired conservatism were much more devoted to limiting government intrusion in
business affairs and expanding the material freedoms of big capital.
Neither the prevailing conservative ferment nor the ethics of private
enterprise exerted any observable restraints on materialism, changing
sexual mores, on the increasingly crude vulgarity of popular culture,
or on the trumpeting of gun ownership as testament to freedom and
virility.

After his presidency, Ronald Reagan became a godlike figure for
American conservatives. With deft and effective use of his acting skills,
he was, indeed, a great communicator of conservative slogans and ideology. But his admirers built a largely fictional mythology about his role.
Much of his more flexible record on taxes, deficits, and social issues like
abortion as governor of California were conveniently stored away and
forgotten. Despite the unyielding tone of his conservative rhetoric, as
president, Ronald Reagan was capable of compromise across party lines,
a disposition apparently lost to conservative Republicans in recent years.
During his two terms in office, his promises of balanced budgets and
smaller government did not materialize. As noted, both the national debt
and the size of the federal government grew substantially. Conservative
memories of these realities dissolved. What survived were conservative
shibboleths and his heroic profile that served to inspire a new generation
of Republican faithful. What followed was an era of growth in
conservative political clout. Conservatism after Reagan was marked by
requisite posturing on social issues and an unstinting defense of
free enterprise backed by a multipronged legislative program of deregulation, the reversal of New Deal initiatives, tax cuts for those who needed

them least, and assaults on economic safety nets for those who needed them most. All this came with the tacit and sometimes active cooperation of cowed and timid Democrats gulled by the myth of deregulation as an economic stimulus and inept at countering right-wing rhetoric. Some Democrats bought into conservative fantasies, other simply wilted. In the face of the conservative political surge, Democrats forgot their history and their obligations.

When Newt Gingrich led the new Republican majority elected to Congress in 1994, he claimed to be leading a populist revolution against special interests. But in fact he and his party conducted "the greatest romp for business interests since the Gilded Age." His program left intact billions in tax breaks and subsidies for big business while proposing cuts in assistance programs for the poor.[10] While the pro-business agenda advanced, issues of importance to another wing of the conservative movement were soft-peddled. Gingrich's highly touted "Contract with America" avoided such issues as abortion and school prayer. Despite the necessary rhetorical flourishes, action on these issues was regarded as too divisive even among conservatives and especially for those of libertarian bent. Gingrich's years of leadership and his "Contract with America" came on with a flourish, but in the end reprised the standard modern conservative agenda of support for the big business goals of deregulation and lower taxes.

It is worth noting that modern conservative propaganda articulated by theorists like Von Mises, Hayek, and Friedman and political leaders like Goldwater, Reagan, and Gingrich repeatedly pounded out the idea that government interference with the free market was a great danger to the very survival of freedom and democracy in America. How democracy and freedom managed to survive in the face of the regulatory regimes of Theodore Roosevelt, Woodrow Wilson, Franklin Roosevelt, Harry Truman, John Kennedy, and Lyndon Johnson conservative eloquence did not effectively explain.

The Gilded Age Revisited

During the first 15 years of this still young century, confusions and contradictions persist in the ranks of those who call themselves conservatives. Big money interests continue and expand their inordinate influence in American politics even as they hear ominous and ironic thunder on the Far Right. The emergence of the Tea Party movement in the last decade signaled a troubling turn to extremism in American politics, but one that corporate America has not been reluctant to support and exploit despite protest chants about the evils of Wall Street. Wall Street does not deem the Tea Party threat serious enough for real concern, but, in fact, finds the movement's mischievous influence on divided government and political gridlock eminently useful. Nothing could be more helpful to corporate aims than government strangled into inactivity. For corporate America an inert and flaccid government is much preferred to one that is active and potent, alert to abuses, and attentive to the well-being of both the consuming and the investing public. Tea Party adherents claim to be enemies of Wall Street even as they trumpet slogans calling for the evisceration of government, a performance for which Wall Street denizens can shout "bravo." In the work of Tea Party types, the big money financial interests see little danger to Wall Street power and great benefit from government paralysis.

While Tea Party shouting about the evils of government has been loud and constant, reducing the effectiveness of government is not a new objective of modern American conservative politics. The history of conservative legislative ideas for over the past 100 years shows an overwhelming majority of conservative efforts have been directed at preventing government action. The record shows many items on national defense and economy in government and much posturing on social issues. But a search for constructive action for needed reforms or adjustments demanded by a society passing through an age that moved from horse-drawn carts to Mars rocket landings is barren. The conservative establishment tried to block even the most moderate conservation and regulatory actions of Theodore Roosevelt and

Woodrow Wilson. Opposition to FDR's New Deal was total and frantic. The modest expansion of social security coverage and raising the minimum wage supported by moderate Republicans under Eisenhower drew the sharpest attacks from the conservative wing of the party. From the Goldwater campaign on, the conservative program has aimed at weakening or undoing civil rights protections, reducing government services and oversight, and the repeated portrayal of government as a barely necessary evil. There is little evidence in the record of the kind of Burkean or Disraeli conservatism that could accept reforming change for the sake of a stable and humane society.

A consistent ideology is difficult to discern in the jumble of Tea Party enthusiasms including an olio of confusions on social issues. They range from concern for order and tradition to a vision of gun ownership as a sacred right. The Tea Party draws many of its supporters from the religious Right, but many others display strong sympathy for libertarianism on cultural as well as political issues. A *New York Times* CBS poll in 2010 showed less than 10 percent difference in the support for both gay marriage and the right to choose abortion between Tea Party supporters and those outside the movement. A Pew Research Center poll in 2011 found 42 percent of Tea Party supporters also supported the conservative Christian movement.[1] The movement's rank and file somehow mix Christian fundamentalist pieties and libertarian individualism.

The movement does, however, uniformly embrace one set of propositions. Tea Partyers equate laissez-faire capitalism with freedom; they despise the federal government, and they especially hate taxes and economic regulation. With an agenda of small government, antiregulation, low taxes, the freest enterprise, and restrictions on labor unions they echo what have been fervent goals of big business lobbies for over a hundred years. Some Tea Party protesters see big business as a great monster, but they champion the smallest possible government, one that would be incapable of imposing any restraints on corporate power. A truly small and weak federal government would leave the already enormous power of financial institutions and giant corporations without even the very modest limits now imposed on megabanks and big business. The Tea Party's hatred of government and its opposition to health-care reform and other progressive ideas "draw on a romanticism of the 'free market' capitalism" that has been embedded in the political culture and constitutes another chapter in the history of market fundamentalism. One Tea Party enthusiast, Michael Leahy, writes that Alexander Hamilton, Herbert Hoover, Franklin Roosevelt, Lyndon Johnson, Richard Nixon, and the senior

George Bush all betrayed the free market that was promised to Americans by the Constitution. In that array of betrayers in the government, political consistency and historical coherence are difficult to discern. His is an interesting and innovative reading of the nation's charter. The object of the Tea Party movement, Leahy's book announces, is to restore the Constitution by ending the regulation of business enterprise.[2]

Tea Party supporters embrace the label "conservative," but they act as extremists, driving moderation out of the Republican Party. Like other conservative and extreme movements on the right, the Tea Party has drawn much financial support from the Koch brothers and their ilk, through front groups like the Americans for Prosperity Foundation and the Scaife family foundations. The Scaife family inherited the wealth of the Andrew Mellon fortune; the Koch Brothers inherited the wealth of their father, Fred Koch, who was one of the founding members of the extremist John Birch Society. A remnant of that group still exists and is Tea Party supportive. Dick Armey's ultra-conservative, business- and free-market-friendly Freedom Works, some of whose money has also come from the Koch family, has offered important stimulus to the growth of Tea Party influence.

In 2004 a group called Citizens for a Sound Economy founded by David Koch merged with a conservative organization called Empower America to form Freedom Works. From the start of Tea Party agitation, Freedom Works helped promote and coordinate dozens of antitax tea parties involving thousands of participants from coast to coast, magnifying the supposed spontaneous "grassroots" character of the movement. Freedom Works has also been a major financial supporter of other Tea Party activities. Freedom Works leaders, Dick Armey and Matt Kibbe, published a Tea Party manifesto in 2010 titled *Give Us Liberty*. Armey resigned as chairman of Freedom Works after a dispute with Kibbe and the board of directors in 2012; Kibbe remains the group's president. In their manifesto they confess the libertarian designs of the Tea Party movement. "Individualism is the unity of purpose that binds the Tea Party movement into a coherent community." Conceding a debt to Ayn Rand, the authors quote Howard Roark, the hero of Rand's novel *Fountainhead*, saying, "Our country, the noblest country in the history of men, was based on the principle of individualism." The book celebrates Rand's libertarian outlook, and Freedom Works distributed copies of *Atlas Shrugged* and other books that support a free-market, individualist philosophy. The economic heroes of Freedom Works are libertarian trio: Friedrich Hayek, Ludwig von Mises, and Milton Friedman. A Wall Street, big bank, big-business champion propagandist could not have assembled a friendlier defense of capitalism than this Freedom Works book that purports to speak for the supposedly grassroots anti–Wall Street Tea Party.[3]

While the Koch brothers and groups like Freedom Works support many of the libertarian notions applauded by Tea Party supporters, they are also the personifications of the inordinate and potentially corrupting power big-business capitalism wields in the American political system. Superrich business sources like the Scaife, Koch, and Coors families and corporate America generally have been more than happy to fund radical movements like the Tea Party in the name of conservatism in order to generate a massive campaign of propaganda in favor of free-market economics undisturbed by public oversight. The resulting encouragement of libertarian causes, financing climate change deniers, undermining of environmental efforts, the steady erosion of consumer protections, the free range of corporate profligacy, and dangerous financial manipulation cannot be squared with the concern for the common good that marked traditional conservatism, but they serve the interests of corporate America very well.

Tea Partyers and others who embrace the label "conservative" dominate the ranks of climate change deniers even in the face of accumulating evidence and scientific consensus. Talk-radio performers like Rush Limbaugh have railed at climate change and environmental issues as some kind of liberal, eggheaded academic conspiracy. Serious environmental action would clearly involve the federal government, would inevitably require public spending, and would necessarily impose restrictions on polluting industries. Each of these is anathema to the current version of conservatism dominant in American politics. That the gullible should accept the talk-radio and lunatic Right distortions of environmental science is very convenient for business interests, some of which regularly fund climate change denying op-ed essays produced by their servile think tanks. That resistance to environmental science and action should pass as conservative is shameful. A genuinely conservative position would look very different. Prudence would dictate action to avoid environmental damage or disaster. Let us assume for argument's sake and against all odds that the science is wrong. What is the worst that would follow from an expansive government program to fight the effects of climate change that did not happen? A good deal of public money would be gone, and corporations would have spent time and resources to meet restrictive regulations. But as the overwhelming evidence suggests, what if climate change performs as the models predict but nothing is done? The national and worldwide disasters following from rising ocean levels, desertification, and increasingly violent weather will cost unimagined numbers of lives and incalculable amounts of money. Given the options, what should be the more prudent, the truly conservative response to the possibility of disastrous climate change? Modern conservatism in the service of capitalist interests, which are almost by definition short-term profit interests, offers little comfort.

Aside from Tea Party and other extremism on the right, another disturbing array of radical ideas labeled "conservative" has come from the American judiciary in recent years. The majority of the U.S. Supreme Court, clearly sailing under a conservative flag, has consistently rendered politically charged decisions in support of the interests of capital. This is especially visible in the enthusiasm of the court majority for eliminating restrictions on the financing of political campaigns. Justices John Roberts, Samuel Alito, Antonin Scalia, Clarence Thomas, and Anthony Kennedy formed the five vote majority in the case of *Citizens United v. the Federal Elections Commission* in 2010, declaring it to be a violation of the First Amendment free speech protection for the government to restrict independent political spending by corporations, associations, and labor unions. This did not alter limits on contributions to specific candidates or parties, but it opened floodgates of spending for indirect but effective support of candidates, parties, and issues. The decision favored the obviously much deeper pockets of corporations and interested billionaires despite its mention of labor unions. Justice Thomas, consistently the most extreme of the conservative justices, concurred in the decision, but he was disappointed that the ruling did not outlaw disclosure requirements along with the limits on spending.

The same five justices again joined as the majority in the case of *McCutcheon v. Federal Elections Commission* in April 2014. That decision effectively removed limits on aggregate contributions by persons giving to multiple campaigns. Though this decision did not affect the limits on giving to a single candidate, Justice Thomas thought it should. He voted with his four conservative colleagues, but also submitted an opinion that limits of any kind on campaign contributions were unconstitutional. These radical decisions, couched in pious language in defense of free speech, added enormous power to the moneyed classes to influence the electoral process. And they come from those justices of the court who are described as conservative. The numberless possibilities for distortions of the political systems and subversion of the democratic process resulting from these decisions are stunning. The dissenting opinion of Justice John Paul Stevens in the Citizens United case focused precisely on the damage the majority decision could do to the appearance of and the potential for corruption in the electoral system.

In its October 11, 2014 edition the *New York Times* reported that a "flood of secret money" coming from groups that do not identify their donors accounted for more than half of the spending on political advertising for that election season. The money was reportedly going disproportionately to Republican candidates and coming from organizations formed to shield wealthy individual and corporate contributors. The *Times* reported that "close to 80 percent of general election advertising by outside groups aiding Republicans has been paid for with secret money, donated by groups like the U.S. Chamber of Commerce, Freedom Partners—a trade association of donors with ties to Charles G. and David H. Koch—and Crossroads GPS, founded by Karl Rove." The opportunities for corporate interests to buy candidates and pervert elections have been hugely expanded in the name of freedom of speech. The already inordinate power of capital to corrupt elections and shape national policy to serve its interests is now magnified with the court's blessing. Add to this the recent conservative Republican efforts in many states to throw obstacles in the way of voter registration clearly aimed at limiting participation in elections by minorities and the poor. Combined with the now virtually limitless opportunities for big money to influence elections, these actions are damaging and dangerous insults to the political system. Self-proclaimed conservative organizations and their cooperative broadcast and print outlets look on and applaud. To call the effects of the court's decisions and the work of voter restriction "conservative" empties the word of meaning. Reactionary would be more appropriate. That conservatives watch and approve what amounts to an assault on the democratic process itself shames the label "conservative."

The collapse of the financial system in 2008 threatened a worldwide crisis and inaugurated what has been dubbed the Great Recession. At this writing, recovery from that disaster is still not fully complete. It is clear from postmortems of the debacle that deregulation contributed greatly to the buccaneer antics of the giant banks in their sophisticated thievery. And the colossal frauds authorized by executives of financial institutions remain largely unpunished. With the exception of the collapse of Lehman Brothers, the giant banks were not weakened by the crisis they caused; they are still dangerous and have actually grown stronger with the help of a government fearful of future bank collapses and instability. "Too big to fail" has not disappeared as a threat to financial stability.

Some halting steps were taken to restore a semblance of regulation to the financial world with the passage of the Dodd-Frank Act. Also known as the Wall Street and Consumer Protection Act, the act was signed by President Obama in July 2010. Among other provisions this extensive and very detailed legislation required more transparency in the marketing of complex derivatives, created an agency to assure clearer information for consumers of securities, and provided new tools to deal with failing financial firms and resulting financial crises. The law was an attempt to reverse the trend of deregulation that had contributed so much to the irresponsibility of the financial industry. Responses to the law were mixed. Supporters of effective regulation did not think it went far enough; conservatives were appalled. Conservative and libertarian organizations like the Federalist Society and the Cato Institute published commentaries hostile to the law for giving the government too much power, and they questioned its constitutionality. It is interesting that the Federalist Society lists among its members Justices Roberts, Scalia, Alito, and Thomas, the four most conservative voices of the Supreme Court. It is also worth noting that in the last 25 years the United States has experienced three financial traumas of painful severity—the savings and loan industry collapse in 1990, the Enron scandal of 2001, and the financial and banking crisis of 2008. In each case the onset of crisis and recession was preceded by a spate of government deregulation and relaxed supervision of financial practices.

With moderates almost entirely driven out of the Republican Party, extremists now dominate the party and exert an influence on the American political system and the government out of proportion to their numbers. That influence during the years of the Obama administration can be legitimately described as obstructionist. If the Right cannot shrink the government, it has demonstrated that it can paralyze federal action, block even the most reasonable and necessary legislation, and call it conservatism.

By the second decade of the twenty-first century, American conservative movements have succeeded in opening the electoral system to corrupt influence, altered the tax code in favor of the already rich, shrunk social safety net provisions, opposed raising of the minimum wage, fought against establishing a responsible national health-care system, dramatically weakened the ability of government to regulate business leading to repeated financial crises and acute recession, and weakened labor unions through right-to-work laws and the action of conservative state governments unfriendly to labor. All these have long sat on the "to-do" list of American corporate capital. This is not a conservative agenda in any meaningful use of the word, but it is clear evidence that capitalism has appropriated conservative language, adherents, and energy to its own service. Despite pious ejaculations and the rhetoric of high moralism, those who pass as conservatives have had little success in implementing the goals of the older tradition of conservatism calling for restored respect for tradition, enduring values, resistance to the continuing vulgarization of American culture, and support for tempered reform. Where has genuine conservatism gone?

Conclusion

Conservatives have associated uncontrolled capitalism with freedom, democracy, and an assortment of other good things. A more objective assessment of the system would argue that capitalist practitioners produce whatever benefits and abuses that come from capitalism and neither are inherent in the system. Capitalism is a system of economic organization. In its basic operation it provides for the investment of private capital in a venture of commerce, manufacturing, or service with the expectation of a return of the capital plus a profit. That is its essential nature. It can be regulated or not; it can exist in a democracy or in a dictatorship. It is not a form of government but an economic system whose fundamental purpose and driving energy derive from producing a profit for investors. It is not tied to any particular religious or ethical system. In these basic terms, it is an amoral system that can function benignly or viciously. It is no more "moral" than chemistry, carpentry, or baseball. Any concepts of justice or moral value must be imposed on the system from the outside, by the choices made by its practitioners, and by the rules imposed by the societies in which it operates. One would hope that sound and just moral principles and civic responsibility always guide capitalists. Most capitalists are probably so guided; many are not. The record of American capitalism for the past 150 years is hardly unblemished. Monopolies choking competition, abuse of workers, fraudulent practices bilking consumers, bribery and corruption of government officials, and even cheating on government contracts during wartime have been a discouragingly large part of the history of American business enterprise. Shoddy goods, unfulfilled specifications, overcharges, and theft have been amply documented for every American conflict from the Civil War to the recent adventures in the Middle East. Patriotism has its limits and is not an inherent characteristic of capitalism as an economic system. It is also clear that these perfidies, motivated by the accumulation of ever greater profits, have been most egregious in those eras that most closely approached free enterprise conditions or relaxed government oversight.

Given the classic conservative view of human nature, the conservative insistence on leaving the capitalist as free as possible does not make sense. Traditionalist conservatives have always believed humans are fallible and prone to antisocial and, too often, to grossly immoral behavior. Why then should we expect all capitalists, left to their own devices, to behave like angels? The logic of the traditional conservative view of human nature should move conservatives to advocate careful supervision and regulation of business activity to prevent abuses and safeguard the common good. Policing huge industries and perfidious entrepreneurs would provide a valuable service to the honest businessman, the consumer, and the society. But modern conservatism, dominated by capitalist self-serving views of government and free enterprise, marches righteously and insistently to the music of the mythical free market. Too many of those few who still see themselves as genuinely traditional conservatives either join the march or watch quietly from the sidelines.

The appropriation of traditional conservatism by capitalist big-business interests distorted conservative thought and created an essentially new movement while retaining the old label. For several centuries capitalist enterprise enjoyed a close economic relationship with government in the mercantilist era. That relationship was marked by myriad annoying regulations imposed by government, but businessmen also enjoyed government protections from foreign competition, and in many cases monopoly privileges in domestic and foreign trade. A monopoly of trade in tea granted to the British East India Company had more than a little to do with sparking turmoil in the American colonies. The relationship between government and business under mercantilism was strategically important, but more than a bit too cozy. Business was dictated to and regulated by government for the perceived interests of the nation. The more prosperous the nation's businesses grew, the greater the tax revenue available to royal government. More national income meant the ability to afford a larger military for defense and for imperial adventure. And, not incidentally, greater income could also support lavish royal digs like Versailles. So mercantilist policy imposed multiple rules and regulation governing foreign trade and domestic production on business ventures with an eye toward increasing national revenue. Until the nineteenth century all Western nations practiced mercantilism; it was the reigning economic orthodoxy. Human fallibility inevitably corrupted the system, and kings, parliaments, and favored businesses worked it to their special advantage. The power of corporations or private capital was not then sufficient to disturb reigning economic theory. Then Adam Smith recognized that too much government control could be stifling and thus touted the benefits of a free market. But he also insisted that the market could be made "unfree" not only by excessive government regulation, but also by the manipulations of the capitalist himself. Smith understood that the size of corporations, as well as collusion, monopoly, and other strategies available to the astute, could distort the market and interfere with the benefits of genuine competition. To check the effect of these, Smith, as noted, saw an important role for government.

Although businessmen at first resisted the laissez-faire ideas of Adam Smith, who prescribed intense competition as best for business and society, capital soon came to see the benefits of cutting the cord to government dependence. Encouraged by Darwinian ideas and the preachers of the Gospel of Wealth, the business community now looked to Smith's *Wealth of Nations*, edited to suit their needs, as an economic scripture of biblical force. In defense of capital, Adam Smith is the most often cited but rarely read. Smith did indeed broadcast a doctrine of free enterprise, but enthusiasts seldom quoted his warnings about market distortions by capital and the important role of government regulation to ensure justice and to keep a free market truly free. The 2014 Nobel Prize for economics was awarded to French economist Jean Tirole for his studies of government regulation of large industries. The clear evidence of his work revealed that industries dominated by a few big corporations, if unregulated, block competition and produce unjustifiable high prices for consumers. Reporting on the Nobel award on October 14, the Associated Press revealed that Tirole attributed the cause of the financial crisis of 2008 principally to the absence of effective government regulation.

Also in 2014, another French economist published a highly acclaimed analysis of the relation of wealth and taxes. Thomas Piketty's highly acclaimed *Capital in the Twenty-First Century* convincingly documented the endemic tendency of capitalism to funnel money disproportionately to the already wealthy. The evidence attached much of the cause for this phenomenon to super-friendly tax policies. Piketty insisted that such income distortion carries a long-term negative impact on the economy and endangers democracy. Predictably, conservative pundits quickly launched editorial attacks on the book and its author.

Gilded Age capitalism embraced the idea of unregulated enterprise, though capitalists were slow to abandon lobbying for government subsidies and tariff protection, and they were more than willing to use their power to distort the free market. The new Gilded Age conservatism cast government as an enemy whose reach should be limited as much as possible. Against that enemy they applied the language of liberty and individual freedom, a style of argument that persists in modern conservative thought and rhetoric. Any deviation, any concession of regulatory functions to government was defined as a step toward socialism and totalitarianism or, in the language of Hayek, the road to serfdom. This conviction remained undisturbed in conservative thought despite the concrete evidence that the interventions of the New Deal of Franklin Roosevelt brought an era of extended growth and prosperity to America and lifted millions of farmers and urban workers into a hugely expanded middle class. If this was serfdom, Tolstoy would not have recognized it. Despite the evidence, for the new conservatism the free market became a magical place. Laissez-faire enterprise, with government largely confined to maintaining law and order, it was confidently asserted, would inevitably bring progress and prosperity to all. This idea served as an article of economic and political faith with scant need for evidence or empirical support.

The embrace of capitalist values and the passionate defense of laissez-faire capitalism are incompatible with classical or traditional conservatism. Traditional conservatism insisted not that change and development in society were bad in themselves, but that core social and cultural values should not be lightly sacrificed to efficiency, novelty, or mere profit. A society's traditions, religious and ethical values, cultural heritage, artistic legacy, concern for others, and economic relations were matters of community interest and community responsibility. Change could be welcome but ought not to do damage. In the modern world, at least since the second half of the nineteenth century, capitalism has become a dominant influence for change with little regard for preservation or continuity and with careless distortion of culture and values, much of it grotesque.

As free enterprise doctrines developed and hardened, differences between the old and the new conservatism festered. As with Smith, Edmund Burke also retained his hero status in the new conservatism, and like Smith he was often praised from afar with little real understanding of his thought. Burke was hardly antigovernment in his conservatism. He was a Whig supporting reforms at home and in the empire, not a Tory in blind defense of aristocratic and royal privilege. As noted, he embraced ideas that were "liberal" for their day. Neither was John Adams, nor several generations of his heirs in the conservative tradition, antigovernment. They certainly did not succumb to the libertarian temptation to defend the actions of a capitalism without limits.

Classic conservatives, then, were not hostile to government. They were determined to resist precipitous, thoughtless changes in established customs and institutions. They hated the mob-think of the kind that sustained the Robespierre radicals of the French Revolution. They were troubled by the increasingly materialist, antireligious direction of Western culture in the nineteenth and twentieth centuries. They were disturbed by the unplanned, thoughtless, often chaotic changes inevitably generated by the rapid and massive expansion of industrial capitalism that was often so costly in human suffering.

What did traditional conservatives want? They desired a well-ordered society that sustained a respect for traditional morals and values. They were open to measured change with clear and controlled focus. They were confident, excessively so, that elite leadership would lead society in the right direction, the historic failure of elite leadership notwithstanding. Liberals, even the elite among them, could embrace the first two, though more easily convinced of the need for change and more open to egalitarianism and democratic practice. These were significant differences, but they did not cast conservatives and liberals as implacable enemies or deny the possibility of cooperation.

What did classic conservatives get from the Gilded Age transformation of the American economic system? The new program, with slogans of free enterprise emblazoned on conservative banners, led with a defense of unrestrained capital at any cost, a program abetted by constant trumpeting of the dangers to life and liberty posed by government regulations that could only lead to socialism and slavery. The new conservatism replaced a healthy resistance to government intrusion into civil liberties with a panicky fear of monster government determined to crush human freedom. The new conservatism also became infected with a mindless libertarian conviction that no codes of conduct, whether prescribed by government, religious institutions, tradition, or common sense, should interfere with absolute individual freedom of action for anything short of warrantless violence. This is in no way compatible with classic conservatism, yet this Randian libertarianism, so useful in its defense of extreme free enterprise, has become an important element in American conservative politics. Rand Paul is no Edmund Burke. He is, however, only one of a legion of recent disciples of the libertarian conservatism of his namesake.

Traditional liberals and conservatives are different but not polar opposites in the political spectrum. Closer to opposites are "reactionaries" and "radicals." Reactionaries not only resist innovation but often seem to wish for a return to the past, a romanticized past that exists only in false recollections and imaginings of a better time now lost. Radicals scoff at tradition and seem ready to plunge ahead with untested theories of utopian reformation. Both are mischievous and dangerous. Historically, as reactionaries and radicals pushed further to the extremes, both seemed, despite the rhetoric of freedom, to arrive at a similarly vicious totalitarianism. Among Hitler, Stalin, and Mao the distinctions among their differences could hardly be appreciated by their millions of victims.

The differences between liberals and conservatives should be most significant in their views of tradition, human nature, and institutional change. Both defend personal freedom; they argue about how much government activism limits that freedom. Both value political and social stability and both value economic justice; their debates should develop over the best means to these ends. In an ideal world, or one might dare to say even in this world, the conservative should admire and perhaps imitate the liberal's sensitivity to injustice (as in the case of racism and the hardships of the working poor), and the liberal should respect and embrace the conservative's prudence in assessing schemes of reform.

In a *Washington Post* column on March 23, 2010, liberal columnist E. J. Dionne expressed his respect and even his affection for conservatives when they challenge progressive reform ideas with hard, practical questions; when they defend the best of tradition; and when they shout "stop" to utopian schemes that are founded more on hopes than reason. The implication of his confession also suggests that conservatives should be more understanding of the liberals' emphasis on equality and on economic well-being necessary to make the enjoyment of freedom possible. When applied to concrete legislation, differences between liberals and conservatives can stimulate heated debate. But in a healthy political system the differences ought more often to concern the pace and degree of change. And on those occasions when disputes focus on irreconcilable policy differences on a particular issue, the conflict ought not to paralyze government. Science, common sense, and rational discussion can direct political consensus on the policies and management of a society organized for the common good. What is necessary for the well-being of a people, for the health of the planet, for stable relations among nations should not lie completely beyond the reach of human reason or political cooperation.

Reaching consensus on these matters, however, is too often diverted and blocked when the political process is corrupted by super-powerful capitalist interests promoting self-serving agendas. The political ideas of the modern version of conservatism were hatched during the Gilded Age, were nurtured through the twentieth century, and have dominated American politics since the Reagan era. The retreat from New Deal benefits and regulatory safeguards and the gridlock in American politics of recent years leaves important demands for government action locked in legislative limbo. The refusal of those who pass as conservatives to cooperate in even the most obviously necessary legislation leaves the government impotent. That condition serves the interests of capitalist entities perfectly well. Meanwhile, the country suffers from the most intense mal-distribution of income since the Gilded Age; the most abusive business practices since the 1920s; the most shameful pockets of inexcusable poverty, especially among children and among the working poor; and the most embarrassing physical deterioration of public facilities in a rich country. If these are the fruits of contemporary conservatism, conservatives should reexamine the original tenets of their traditional faith and consider how and by whom that ideology has been distorted for very unconservative purposes. In the twenty-first century, genuine conservatives should ask, "Who stole conservatism?"

Epilogue—Election Season

As this is written, the scramble is on for the Republican presidential nomination. The performances of the array of candidates confirm the profound confusion that plagues conservatism in modern American politics. As spring approached the large field narrowed, but the posture of the candidates had become clear. All the Republican candidates hustled to identify themselves loudly and often as conservatives, and they tried to outdo each other in establishing their bona fide conservative credentials. To do this they felt compelled to appeal to the extreme wing of the party, to what has tellingly come to be called the Republican base. The common theme sustained by all the candidates was that government itself is a negative force in society and its functions should be cut as deeply and quickly as possible. That posture is the expression of what has been the Republican Party's continuing obstructionism during the two terms of the Obama administration. Despite accumulating evidence of wealth inequality favoring the very rich, cutting taxes even further stood prominently in all the official campaign sites. Repealing the Obama health-care program showed up in the campaign sites and in the candidates' oratory, though what would replace coverage for millions if Obamacare were undone was not made clear. This longing for government inertia fits the aims of big business very well, but the picture does not reflect the traditional conservative profile.

Through the autumn of 2015, the one consistency in repeated polling by various organizations was the firm hold of support for Donald Trump at about 25 to 30 percent. Other candidates trailed behind, with the so-called establishment candidate, Jeb Bush, able to claim only an embarrassing single-digit number in the polls. Neither real estate developer Trump nor neurosurgeon Ben Carson had said very much about concrete issues (with the exception of Trump's xenophobic assault on Latino immigrants and Muslims). This seemed not to dampen the enthusiasm of the most extreme Tea Party troops among the Republicans, nor did it weaken Trumps numbers among almost a third of prospective Republican voters.

Donald Trump has been the delight of all the news media, the serious and the comic. With encouragement from his sensational proclamations and campaign antics, the coverage of Trump has been expansive and constant. One could argue with plausibility that the massive coverage itself has boosted his popularity. Some of his popularity and support seem to come from Far Right and Tea Party sympathizers, but clearly his support is broad among conservatives generally. It is also telling that at one point in the fall polling, he and Carson, both outsiders and neither with any governing experience, commanded the support of almost half of those polled. Decades of conservative chanting that government is the problem could plausibly be deemed to have taken effect. Indeed much editorial and pundit explanations for Trump's appeal pointed to his standing as an outsider and a flaming critic of the governing establishment. Fabrications, distortions, vulgarities, and real-issue emptiness seem to have no effect in diminishing his poll numbers. It is true that his polling ranging from 20 to 35 percent of potential Republican voters represented a small minority of the total national voting population, but it did represent a significant number of voters who have been persuaded, even contrary to their own self-interest, that government is a negative force in the society. Fed by money contributed by the wealthiest representatives of the capitalist establishment, these extreme conservatives play directly into the hands of the similarly financed business lobbies. Conservatives attack government and the Tea Party faithful among them spout obscure and ineffective attacks on big business; Republican presidential hopefuls applaud dutifully, and Wall Street smiles.

While the other candidates tried to distance themselves from Trump's more outlandish claims, they bought into the antigovernment narrative. They all ran scared, careful not to offend the extreme elements of the party. That extreme may include a minority of the party, but it is large enough, energized, and strategically located to influence the outcome of caucus and primary contests. Of this the candidates were keenly aware.

As the full roster of candidates joined a chorus of antigovernment rhetoric, the same thinking was also reflected in the willingness of the most conservative representatives in Congress to see the government shut down despite painful consequences for the economy and for the lives of millions. When finally a compromise was hammered out between the Obama administration and Republicans in the House pressed into agreement by the new Speaker Paul Ryan, Tea Party people were disappointed and angry. It was the absolute refusal of many conservatives in the House to entertain any compromise even at the risk of shutting down the government and paralyzing many essential functions that finally drove Speaker John Boehner to resign in despair.

In addition to cutting the scope and effectiveness of the federal government, the health of the nation seemed to depend, according to campaign slogans, on lowering taxes even on the highest incomes of the famed "one percent." In a *New York Times* column on November 13, Paul Krugman pointed out that there should be no surprise about this position. He noted that the primary candidates received most of their campaign monies from a few very wealthy families. Krugman added that "decades of indoctrination have made an essentially religious faith in the virtues of high-end tax cuts—a faith impervious to evidence—a central part of Republican identity."

All the candidates employed "NRA-Speak" touting unfettered access to guns as the surest defense of freedom in spite of new gun slaughters reported almost weekly. That defending the possession of firearms of great destructive power should be available to all without even the most minimal regulation or control should be a test of conservative commitment is stunning.

The whole of the primary campaign run-up to the election season showed the greatest reluctance among the cast of hopefuls to offer the least offence or to appear to deviate significantly from the sentiments of the most intensely conservative end of the party. Despite the bitterness of the campaign, a visit to their official campaign sites online showed unanimity on issues that have defined modern American conservatism. All supported lower taxes, with no indication that the benefits in this area have gone disproportionately to the very rich, all opposed even modest limits or were mute on the question of gun control, all wanted balanced budgets, fewer business regulations, and all seemed to see an active government as dangerous.

A selection of promises from official campaign sites says something about conservatism in modern American politics. Other sites followed a similar pattern. The following are quotes from the sites.

Donald Trump

> No business of any size, from a Fortune 500 to a mom and pop shop to a freelancer living job to job, will pay more than 15% of their business

income in taxes. This lower rate makes corporate inversions unnecessary by making America's tax rate one of the best in the world.

Ben Carson

We must ratify a Balanced Budget Amendment to the Constitution in order to restore fiscal responsibility to the federal government's budget.

I cannot and will not support any efforts to weaken The 2nd Amendment.

The 2nd Amendment is a central pillar of our Constitution.

Rand Paul

As your President, I will ensure that real free-market principles are applied to the American health care system so that it is responsive to patients, families, and doctors, rather than government bureaucracy.

Counteracting excessively burdensome government regulations has become a centerpiece of my tenure in Washington. All my actions seek to find a balance between environmental, safety and health protection, without compromising the ability of family businesses to flourish.

As President, I vow to uphold our entire Bill of Rights, but specifically our right to bear arms.

Mike Huckabee

As President I will abolish the IRS.

The Second Amendment is the last line of defense against tyranny and must be protected.

Ted Cruz

Cruz has spent his entire life fighting passionately for Limited Government, Economic Growth, and the Constitution.

Marco Rubio

Cut taxes for all businesses to 25 percent.

Put a ceiling on the amount U.S. regulations can cost our economy.

Jeb Bush

First, we have to confront and end the habitual practice of deficit spending. As long as deficits are an option, deficits will be the reality. The remedy that I will support as president is a balanced budget amendment. To be clear, a properly-designed amendment must be a tool to limit government—not raise taxes.

We will cut individual rates from seven brackets to three: 28%, 25% and 10%. At 28%, the highest tax bracket would return to where it was when President Ronald Reagan signed into law his monumental and successful 1986 tax reform.

The core commitment of conservatism to serve the interests of laissez-faire capitalism has not changed significantly since the nineteenth century and is not likely to in the foreseeable future. The ties between American political conservatism and the freest of free enterprise capitalism persist, but they have long since failed to reflect the traditional goals and the real meaning of conservatism in its original incarnation.

Appendix

From the William McKinley to Ronald Reagan, American conservatism assumed a different character and purpose. Key statements in this transformation chronicle the shift from the kind of conservatism associated with Edmund Burk and John Adams to a conservatism dedicated to the service of capital. The following are four enunciations of the values of modern American conservatism.

A. WILLIAM GRAHAM SUMNER ON WEALTH AND POVERTY

William Graham Sumner offers Social Darwinian understanding of wealth and poverty. For him both are products of the evolutionary process, and no adjustments should be made by intrusive government. Neither should the sentimentality of long-cherished but mistaken concern for the poor be taken seriously.

1. There is an old ecclesiastical prejudice in favor of the poor and against the rich. In days when men acted by ecclesiastical rules these prejudices produced waste of capital, and helped mightily to replunge Europe into barbarism. The prejudices are not yet dead, but they survive in our society as ludicrous contradictions and inconsistencies. One thing must be granted to the rich: they are good-natured. Perhaps they do not recognize themselves, for a rich man is even harder to define than a poor one. It is not uncommon to hear a clergyman utter from the pulpit all the old prejudice in favor of the poor and against the rich, while asking the rich to do something for the poor; and the rich comply, without apparently having their feelings hurt at all by the invidious comparison. We all agree that he is a good member of society who works his way up from poverty to wealth, but as soon as he has worked his way up we begin to regard him with suspicion, as a dangerous member of society. A newspaper starts the silly fallacy that "the rich are rich because the poor are industrious," and it is copied from one end of the country to the other as if it were a brilliant apothegm. "Capital" is denounced by writers and speakers who have never taken the trouble to find out what capital is, and who use the word in two or three different senses in as many pages. Labor organizations are formed, not to employ combined effort for a common object, but to indulge in declamation and denunciation, and especially to furnish an easy living to some officers who do not want to work. People who have rejected dogmatic religion, and retained only a residuum of religious sentimentalism, find a special field in the discussion of the rights of the poor and the duties of the rich. We have denunciations of banks, corporations, and monopolies, which denunciations encourage only helpless rage and animosity, because they are not controlled by any definitions or limitations, or by any distinctions between what is indispensably necessary and what is abuse, between what is established in the order of nature and what is legislative error. Think, for instance, of a journal which makes it its special business to denounce monopolies, yet favors a protective tariff, and has not a word to say against trades-unions or patents! Think of public teachers who say that the farmer is ruined by the cost of transportation, when they mean that he cannot make any profits because his farm is too far from the market, and who denounce the railroad because it does not correct for the farmer, at the expense of its stockholders, the disadvantage which lies in the physical situation of the farm! Think of that construction of this situation which attributes all the trouble to the greed of "moneyed corporations!" Think of the piles of rubbish that one has read about corners, and watering stocks, and selling futures!

* * *

All the denunciations and declamations which have been referred to are made in the interest of "the poor man." His name never ceases to echo in the halls of legislation, and he is the excuse and reason for all the acts which are passed. He is never forgotten in poetry, sermon, or essay. His interest is invoked to defend every doubtful procedure and every questionable institution. Yet where is he? Who is he? Who ever saw him? When did he ever get the benefit of any of the numberless efforts in his behalf? When, rather, was his name and interest ever invoked, when, upon examination, it did not plainly appear that somebody else was to win—somebody who was far too "smart" ever to be poor, far too lazy ever to be rich by industry and economy?

* * *

The aggregation of large fortunes is not at all a thing to be regretted. On the contrary, it is a necessary condition of many forms of social advance. If we should set a limit to the accumulation of wealth, we should say to our most valuable producers, "We do not want you to do us the services which you best understand how to perform, beyond a certain point." It would be like killing off our generals in war.

* * *

There is every indication that we are to see new developments of the power of aggregated capital to serve civilization, and that the new developments will be made right here in America. Joint-stock companies are yet in their infancy, and incorporated capital, instead of being a thing which can be overturned, is a thing which is becoming more and more indispensable. I shall have something to say in another chapter about the necessary checks and guarantees, in a political point of view, which must be established. Economically speaking, aggregated capital will be more and more essential to the performance of our social tasks. Furthermore, it seems to me certain that all aggregated capital will fall more and more under personal control. Each great company will be known as controlled by one master mind. The reason for this lies in the great superiority of personal management over management by boards and committees. This tendency is in the public interest, for it is in the direction of more satisfactory responsibility. The great hinderance to the development of this continent has lain in the lack of capital. The capital which we have had has been wasted by division and dissipation, and by injudicious applications. The waste of capital, in proportion to the total capital, in this country between 1800 and 1850, in the attempts which were made to establish means of communication and transportation, was enormous. The waste was chiefly due to ignorance and bad management, especially to State control of public works. We are to see the development of the country pushed forward at an unprecedented rate by an aggregation of capital, and a systematic application of it under the direction of competent men. This development will be for the benefit of all, and it will enable each one of us, in his measure and way, to increase his wealth. We may each of us go ahead to do so, and we have every reason to rejoice in each other's prosperity. There ought to be no laws to guarantee property against the folly of its possessors. In the absence of such laws, capital inherited by a spendthrift will be squandered and re-accumulated in the hands of men who are fit and competent to hold it. So it should be, and under such a state of things there is no reason to desire to limit the property which any man may acquire.

Source: William Graham Sumner, *What Social Classes Owe to Each Other* (New York: Harper & Brothers, 1883).

2. The concentration of wealth I understand to include the aggregation of wealth into large masses, and its concentration under the control of a few.

In this sense the concentration of wealth is indispensable to the successful execution of the tasks which devolve upon society in our time. Every task of society requires the application of capital, and involves an economic problem in the form of the most expedient application of material means to ends. Two features most prominently distinguish the present age from all which have preceded it; those are, first, the great scale on which all societal undertakings must be carried out; second, the transcendent importance of competent management—that is, of the personal element in direction and control. . . .

Stated in the concisest terms the phenomenon is that of a more perfect integration of all societal functions. The concentration of power (wealth), more dominant control, intenser discipline, and stricter methods are but modes of securing more perfect integration. When we perceive this we see that the concentration of wealth is but one feature of a grand step in societal evolution. . . .

No man can acquire a million without helping a million men to increase their little fortunes all the way down through all the social grades. In some points of view it is an error that we fix our attention so much upon the very rich and overlook the prosperous mass, but the compensating advantage is that the great successes stimulate emulation the most powerfully.

What matters it then that some millionaires are idle, or silly, or vulgar, that their ideas are sometimes futile, and their plans grotesque, when they turn aside from money-making? How do they differ in this from any other class? The millionaires are a product of natural selection, acting on the whole body of men, to pick out those who can meet the requirement of certain work to be done. In this respect they are just like the great statesmen, or scientific men, or military men. It is because. It is because they are thus selected that wealth aggregates under their hands both their own and that intrusted to them. Let one of them make a mistake and see how quickly the concentration gives way to dispersion. They may fairly be regarded as the naturally selected agents of society for certain work. They get high wages and live in luxury, but the bargain is a good one for society. There is the intensest competition for this function will be employed in it, so that the cost of it will be reduced to the lowest terms, and furthermore that the competitors will study the proper conduct to be observed in their occupation. This will bring discipline and the correction of arrogance and masterfulness.

Source: William Graham Sumner, "The Concentration of Wealth: Its Economic Justification" (1902), reprinted in *The Challenge of the Facts and Other Essays* (New Haven: Yale University Press, 1914).

~~~

B. HERBERT HOOVER ON RUGGED INDIVIDUALISM AND THE ROLE OF GOVERNMENT

During a presidential election campaign speech on October 22, 1928, Herbert Hoover proclaimed his philosophy of government, which he termed American-ism. He drew on his 1920 essay "American Individualism" to explain his reading of American tradition and the dangers of straying from that philosophy of individualism and restrained government.

This campaign now draws near to a close. The platforms of the two parties defining principles and offering solutions of various national problems have been presented and are being earnestly considered by our people.

After four months' debate it is not the Republican Party which finds reason for abandonment of any of the principles it has laid down or of the views it has expressed for solution of the problems before the country. The principles to which it adheres are rooted deeply in the foundations of our national life and the solutions which it proposed are based on experience with government and a consciousness that it may have the responsibility for placing those solutions into action.

* * *

After the war, when the Republican Party assumed administration of the country, we were faced with the problem of determination of the very nature of our national life. Over 150 years we have builded up a form of self-government and we had builded up a social system which is peculiarly our own. It differs fundamentally from all others in the world. It is the American system. It is just as definite and positive a political and social system as has ever been developed on earth. It is founded upon the conception that self-government can be preserved only by decentralization of Government in the State and by fixing local responsibility; but further than this, it is founded upon the social conception that only through ordered liberty, freedom and equal opportunity to the individual will his initiative and enterprise drive the march of progress.

During the war we necessarily turned to the Government to solve every difficult economic problem. The Government having absorbed every energy of our people to war there was no other solution. For the preservation of the State the Government became a centralized despotism which undertook responsibilities, assumed powers, exercised rights, and took over the business of citizens. To large degree we regimented our whole people temporarily into a socialistic state. However justified it was in time of war if continued in peace time it would destroy not only our system but progress and freedom in our own country and throughout the world. When the war closed the most vital of all issues was whether Governments should continue war ownership and operation of many instrumentalities of production and distribution. We were challenged with the choice of the American system "rugged individualism" or the choice of a European system of diametrically opposed doctrines—doctrines of paternalism and state socialism. The acceptance of these ideas meant the destruction of self-government through centralization of government; it meant the undermining of initiative and enterprise upon which our people have grown to unparalleled greatness.

The Democratic administration cooperated with the Republican Party to demobilize many of her activities and the Republican Party from the beginning of its period of power resolutely turned its face away from these ideas and these war practices, back to our fundamental conception of the state and the rights and responsibilities of the individual. Thereby it restored confidence and hope in the American people, it freed and stimulated enterprise, it restored the Government to its position as an umpire instead of a player in the economic game. For these reasons the American people have gone forward in progress while the rest of the world is halting and some countries have even gone backwards. If anyone will study the causes which retarded recuperation of Europe, he will find much of it due to the stifling of private initiative on one hand, and overloading of the Government with business on the other.

I regret, however, to say that there has been revived in this campaign a proposal which would be a long step to the abandonment of our American system, to turn to the idea of government in business. Because we are faced with difficulty and doubt over certain national problems which we are faced—that is prohibition, farm relief and electrical power—our opponents propose that we must to some degree thrust government into these businesses and in effect adopt state socialism as a solution.

There is, therefore submitted to the American people the question— Shall we depart from the American system and start upon a new road. And I wish to emphasize this question on this occasion. I wish to make clear my position on the principles involved for they go to the very roots of American life in every act of our Government. I should like to state to you the effect of the extension of government into business upon our system of self-government and our economic system. But even more important is the effect upon the average man. That is the effect on the very basis of liberty and freedom not only to those left outside the fold of expanded bureaucracy but to those embraced within it.

When the Federal Government undertakes a business, the state governments are at once deprived of control and taxation of that business; when the state government undertakes a business it at once deprived the municipalities of taxation and control of that business. Business requires centralization; self-government requires decentralization. Our government to succeed in business must become in effect a despotism. There is thus at once an insidious destruction of self-government.

* * *

Liberalism [Hoover uses the term here in its nineteenth-century usage applied to economics.] is a force truly of the spirit, a force proceeding from the deep realization that economic freedom cannot be sacrificed if political freedom is to be preserved. Even if governmental conduct of business could give us more efficiency instead of giving us decreased efficiency, the fundamental objection to it would remain unaltered and unabated. It would destroy political equality. It would cramp and cripple mental and spiritual energies of our people. It would dry up the spirit of liberty and progress. It would extinguish equality of opportunity, and for these reasons fundamentally and primarily it must be resisted. For a hundred and fifty years liberalism has found its true spirit in the American system, not in the European systems.

* * *

Our people have the right to know whether we can continue to solve our great problems without abandonment of our American system. I know we can. We have demonstrated that our system is responsive enough to meet any new and intricate development in our economic and business life. We have demonstrated that we can maintain our democracy as master in its own house and that we can preserve equality of opportunity and individual freedom.

One of the great problems of government is to determine to what extent the Government itself shall interfere with commerce and industry and how much it shall leave to individual exertion. It is just as important that business keep out of government as that government keep out of business. No system is perfect. We have had abuses in the conduct of business that every good citizen resents. But I insist that the results show our system better than any other and retains the essentials of freedom.

* * *

There is a still further road to progress which is consonant with our American system—a method that reinforces our individualism by reducing, not increasing, Government interference in business.

Source: Herbert Hoover, "Principles and Ideals of the United States Government." Speech given October 22, 1928. Available online at http://millercenter.org/president/speeches/speech-6000.

~~~

C. REPUBLICAN PARTY PLATFORM OF 1936

By 1936 the bipartisan liberalism of the first decades of the century was gone; progressives had abandoned the Republican Party, and conservatives were in full control. The platform crafted at the party convention read Roosevelt's New Deal efforts against the Depression as a disaster and promised a return to sound government. The electorate disagreed.

America is in peril. The welfare of American men and women and the future of our youth are at stake. We dedicate ourselves to the preservation of their political liberty, their individual opportunity and their character as free citizens, which today for the first time are threatened by Government itself.

- For three long years the New Deal Administration has dishonored American traditions and flagrantly betrayed the pledges upon which the Democratic Party sought and received public support.
- The powers of Congress have been usurped by the President.
- The integrity and authority of the Supreme Court have been flouted.
- The rights and liberties of American citizens have been violated.
- Regulated monopoly has displaced free enterprise.
- The New Deal Administration constantly seeks to usurp the rights reserved to the States and to the people.
- It has insisted on the passage of laws contrary to the Constitution.
- It has intimidated witnesses and interfered with the right of petition.

- It has dishonored our country by repudiating its most sacred obligations.
- It has been guilty of frightful waste and extravagance, using public funds for partisan political purposes.
- It has promoted investigations to harass and intimidate American citizens, at the same time denying investigations into its own improper expenditures.
- It has created a vast multitude of new offices, filled them with its favorites, set up a centralized bureaucracy, and sent out swarms of inspectors to harass our people.
- It has bred fear and hesitation in commerce and industry, thus discouraging new enterprises, preventing employment and prolonging the depression.
- It secretly has made tariff agreements with our foreign competitors, flooding our markets with foreign commodities.
- It has coerced and intimidated voters by withholding relief to those opposing its tyrannical policies. It has coerced and intimidated voters by withholding relief to those opposing its policies.
- It has destroyed the morale of our people and made them dependent upon government.
- Appeals to passion and class prejudice have replaced reason and tolerance.
- To a free people, these actions are insufferable. This campaign cannot be waged on the traditional differences between the Republican and Democratic parties. The responsibility of this election transcends all previous political divisions. We invite all Americans, irrespective of party, to join us in defense of American institutions.

Constitutional Government and Free Enterprise

We pledge ourselves:

1. To maintain the American system of Constitutional and local self government, and to resist all attempts to impair the authority of the Supreme Court of the United States, the final protector of the rights of our citizens against the arbitrary encroachments of the legislative and executive branches of government. There can be no individual liberty without an independent judiciary.
2. To preserve the American system of free enterprise, private competition, and equality of opportunity, and to seek its constant betterment in the interests of all.

Reemployment

The only permanent solution of the unemployment problem is the absorption of the unemployed by industry and agriculture. To that end, we advocate:

- Removal of restrictions on production. Abandonment of all New Deal policies that raise production costs, increase the cost of living, and thereby restrict buying, reduce volume and prevent reemployment.
- Encouragement instead of hindrance to legitimate business.
- Withdrawal of government from competition with private payrolls.
- Elimination of unnecessary and hampering regulations.
- Adoption of such other policies as will furnish a chance for individual enterprise, industrial expansion, and the restoration of jobs.

Relief

The necessities of life must be provided for the needy, and hope must be restored pending recovery. The administration of relief is a major failing of the New Deal. It has been faithless to those who must deserve our sympathy. To end confusion, partisanship, waste and incompetence, we pledge:

1. The return of responsibility for relief administration to non-political local agencies familiar with community problems.
2. Federal grants-in-aid to the States and territories while the need exists, upon compliance with these conditions: (a) a fair proportion of the total relief burden to be provided from the revenues of States and local governments; (b) all engaged in relief administration to be selected on the basis of merit and fitness; (c) adequate provision to be made for the encouragement of those persons who are trying to become self-supporting.
3. Undertaking of Federal public works only on their merits and separate from the administration of relief.
4. A prompt determination of the facts concerning relief and unemployment.

* * *

Regulation of Business

We recognize the existence of a field within which governmental regulation is desirable and salutary. The authority to regulate should be vested in an independent tribunal acting under clear and specific laws establishing definite standards. Their determinations on law and facts should be subject to review by the Courts. We favor Federal regulation, within the Constitution, of the marketing of securities to protect investors. We favor also Federal regulation of the interstate activities of public utilities.

* * *

Government Finance

The New Deal Administration has been characterized by shameful waste, and general financial irresponsibility. It has piled deficit upon deficit. It threatens national bankruptcy and the destruction through inflation of insurance policies and savings bank deposits. We pledge ourselves to:

> Stop the folly of uncontrolled spending. Balance the budget—not by increasing taxes but by cutting expenditures, drastically and immediately.
> Revise the federal tax system and coordinate it with state and local tax systems.
> Use the taxing power for raising revenue and not for punitive or political purposes.

* * *

Conclusion

We assume the obligations and duties imposed upon Government by modern conditions. We affirm our unalterable conviction that, in the future as in the past, the fate of the nation will depend, not so much on the wisdom and power of government, as on the character and virtue, self-reliance, industry and thrift of the people and on their willingness to meet the responsibilities essential to the preservation of a free society.

* * *

Source: Republican Party Platforms, "Republican Party Platform of 1936," June 9, 1936. Online by Gerhard Peters and John T. Woolley, The American Presidency Project. http://www.presidency.ucsb.edu/ws/?pid=29639.

<div align="center">~~~</div>

D. RONALD REAGAN INAUGURAL

In January 1981, the new president launched a new era of conservative governance reiterating what had become core modern American conservative creed. These included lower taxes, a balanced budget, freer enterprise, individualism, and government as the problem. All seemed to be linked as essential for the preservation of freedom.

* * *

The business of our nation goes forward. These United States are confronted with an economic affliction of great proportions. We suffer from the longest and one of the worst sustained inflations in our national history. It distorts our economic decisions, penalizes thrift, and crushes the struggling young and the fixed-income elderly alike. It threatens to shatter the lives of millions of our people.

Idle industries have cast workers into unemployment, human misery, and personal indignity. Those who do work are denied a fair return for their labor by a tax system which penalizes successful achievement and keeps us from maintaining full productivity.

But great as our tax burden is, it has not kept pace with public spending. For decades we have piled deficit upon deficit, mortgaging our future and our children's future for the temporary convenience of the present. To continue this long trend is to guarantee tremendous social, cultural, political, and economic upheavals.

You and I, as individuals, can, by borrowing, live beyond our means, but for only a limited period of time. Why, then, should we think that collectively, as a nation, we're not bound by that same limitation? We must act today in order to preserve tomorrow. And let there be no misunderstanding: We are going to begin to act, beginning today.

The economic ills we suffer have come upon us over several decades. They will not go away in days, weeks, or months, but they will go away. They will go away because we as Americans have the capacity now, as we've had in the past, to do whatever needs to be done to preserve this last and greatest bastion of freedom.

In this present crisis, government is not the solution to our problem; government is the problem. From time to time we've been tempted to believe that society has become too complex to be managed by self-rule, that government by an elite group is superior to government for, by, and of the people. Well, if no one among us is capable of governing himself, then who among us has the capacity to govern someone else? All of us together, in and out of government, must bear the burden. The solutions we seek must be equitable, with no one group singled out to pay a higher price.

* * *

So, as we begin, let us take inventory. We are a nation that has a government—not the other way around. And this makes us special among the nations of the Earth. Our government has no power except that granted it by the people. It is time to check and reverse the growth of government, which shows signs of having grown beyond the consent of the governed.

It is my intention to curb the size and influence of the Federal establishment and to demand recognition of the distinction between the powers granted to the Federal Government and those reserved to the States or to the people. All of us need to be reminded that the Federal Government did not create the States; the States created the Federal Government.

Now, so there will be no misunderstanding, it's not my intention to do away with government. It is rather to make it work—work with us, not over us; to stand by our side, not ride on our back. Government can and must provide opportunity, not smother it; foster productivity, not stifle it.

If we look to the answer as to why for so many years we achieved so much, prospered as no other people on Earth, it was because here in this land we unleashed the energy and individual genius of man to a greater extent than has ever been done before. Freedom and the dignity of the individual have been more available and assured here than in any other place on Earth. The price for this freedom at times has been high, but we have never been unwilling to pay that price.

It is no coincidence that our present troubles parallel and are proportionate to the intervention and intrusion in our lives that result from unnecessary and excessive growth of government. It is time for us to realize that we're too great a nation to limit ourselves to small dreams. We're not, as some would have us believe, doomed to an inevitable decline. I do not believe in a fate that will fall on us no matter what we do. I do believe in a fate that will fall on us if we do nothing. So, with all the creative energy at our command, let us begin an era of national renewal. Let us renew our determination, our courage, and our strength. And let us renew our faith and our hope.

* * *

In the days ahead I will propose removing the roadblocks that have slowed our economy and reduced productivity. Steps will be taken aimed at restoring the balance between the various levels of government. Progress may be slow, measured in inches and feet, not miles, but we will progress. It is time to reawaken this industrial giant, to get government back within its means, and to lighten our punitive tax burden. And these will be our first priorities, and on these principles there will be no compromise.

Source: Ronald Reagan, "Inaugural Address," January 20, 1981. Online by Gerhard Peters and John T. Woolley, *The American Presidency Project.* http://www.presidency.ucsb.edu/ws/?pid=43130.

Notes

CHAPTER 1

1. Burke, Edmund, *Reflections on the Revolution in France* (New York: Oxford University Press, 1993), 22.

2. Ibid., 196.

3. Ibid., 111–113.

4. Ibid., 49, 52, 258.

5. Ibid., 169–170.

6. Ibid., 97–98.

7. Ibid., 33.

8. Ibid., 90–91.

9. Mansfield, Harvey C., *Selected Letters of Edmund Burke* (Chicago: University of Chicago Press, 1984), 257.

10. Quoted in Ker, Ian, *John Henry Newman* (New York: Oxford University Press, 1990), 721.

11. Martin, Brian, *John Henry Newman* (New York: Oxford University Press, 1982), 144.

12. Newman, John Henry, *The Idea of a University* (New Haven: Yale University Press, 1996), 89.

CHAPTER 2

1. Wood, Gordon, *Empire for Liberty* (New York: Oxford University Press, 2009), 147; Rossiter, Clinton, *Conservatism in America* (New York: Vintage Books, 1962), 108–109.

2. Smith, Page, *John Adams* (Garden City, NY: Doubleday & Company, 1962), 107–108.

3. McCullough, David, *John Adams* (New York: Simon and Schuster, 2001), 69–70; Smith, *John Adams*, 503.

4. Current, Richard N., *Daniel Webster and the Rise of National Conservatism* (Boston: Little Brown and Co., 1955), 193–195; Wilentz, Sean, *The Rise of American Democracy* (New York: W. W. Norton, 2005), 484–485.

5. Schlesinger, Arthur M., Jr., *The Age of Jackson* (Boston: Little Brown and Co., 1953), 405; Gabriel, Ralph Henry, *The Course of American Democratic Thought* (New York: The Ronald Press, 1956), 57; Kirk, Russell, *The Conservative Mind* (Chicago: Regenery Books, 1986), 246.

6. Adams, Henry, *The Education of Henry Adams* (New York: Random House, 1931), 500; Stevenson, Elizabeth, ed., *A Henry Adams Reader* (Garden City, NY: Doubleday & Company, 1958), 85–86.

7. Ford, Worthington Chauncey, ed., *Letters of Henry Adams 1892–1918* (Boston: Houghton Mifflin Company, 1938), 111; Donovan, Timothy Paul, *Henry and Brooks Adams* (Norman: University of Oklahoma Press, 1961), 169, 272; Adams, *Education*, 500.

8. Adams, Brooks, *The Theory of Social Revolutions* (New York: The Macmillan Company, 1913), 209–210, 213, 215; Donovan, *Henry and Brooks Adams*, 168; Adams, Brooks, 295–296, 227.

CHAPTER 3

1. *The Constitution of the United States of America Analysis and Interpretation* (Washington, D.C.: Government Printing Office, 1964), 1281; Beth, Loren P., *The Development of the American Constitution* (New York: Harper & Row, 1971), 173.

2. McCloskey, Robert G., *American Conservatism in the Age of Enterprise 1865–1910* (New York: Harper & Row, 1964), 50.

3. Carnegie, Andrew, *The Gospel of Wealth and Other Timely Essays* (Cambridge: Harvard University Press, 1962), 16.

4. Ibid., 25, 28, 49.

5. Goldman, Eric F., *Rendezvous with Destiny* (New York: Vintage Books/Knopf, 1956), 69.

6. Conwell, Russell H., *Acres of Diamonds* (New York: Harper & Brothers, 1915), 18, 20, 21.

7. Smith, Adam, *The Wealth of Nations* (New York: Random House, 1937), 61, 123–129, 777.

8. Lash, Christopher, *The Culture of Narcissism* (New York: W. W. Norton, 1979), 395.

9. Kirk, Russell, *The Conservative Mind* (Chicago: Regenery Books, 1986), 373; Scruton, Roger, *The Meaning of Conservatism* (Totowa, NJ: Barnes and Noble Books, 1980), 95, 109–110.

CHAPTER 4

1. Rossiter, Clinton, *Conservatism in America* (New York: Vintage Books, 1962), 131.
2. DiNunzio, Mario R., *Franklin Roosevelt and the Third American Revolution* (Santa Barbara, CA: Praeger, 2011), 29, 65.
3. Leuchtenburg, William E., *Franklin D. Roosevelt and the New Deal* (New York: Harper & Row, 1963), 176.
4. Schlesinger, Arthur M., Jr., *The Politics of Upheaval* (Boston: Houghton Mifflin Company, 1960), 500.
5. Schlesinger, Arthur M., Jr., *The Coming of the New Deal* (Boston: Houghton Mifflin Company, 1959), 473.
6. Leuchtenburg, William E., ed., *The New Deal* (New York: Harper & Row, 1968), 197.
7. Ibid., 205.
8. Kennedy, David M., *Freedom from Fear* (New York: Oxford University Press, 1999), 340.

CHAPTER 5

1. Rossiter, Clinton, *Conservatism in America* (New York: Vintage Books, 1962), 211.
2. Twelve Southerners, *I'll Take My Stand* (Baton Rouge: Louisiana State University Press, 1977), 147.
3. Weaver, Richard M., *Ideas Have Consequences* (Chicago: University of Chicago Press), 1984, 132–133.
4. Smith, Ted J., III, ed., *In Defense of Tradition, Collected Shorter Writing of Richard M. Weaver* (Indianapolis: Liberty Fund, 2000), 482.
5. Genovese, Eugene D., *The Southern Tradition* (Cambridge: Harvard University Press, 1994), 83, 99, 102.
6. Viereck, Peter, *Conservatism Revisited* (New York: The Free Press, 1962), 17, 32, 134–137.
7. Scruton, Roger, *The Meaning of Conservatism* (Totowa, NJ: Barnes and Noble Books, 1980), 95, 105, 109–110; Oakeshott, Michael, *Rationalism in Politics* (New York: Basic Books, 1962), 55.
8. Kirk, Russell, *The Conservative Mind* (Chicago: Regenery Books, 1986), 45; Kirk, Russell, *Edmund Burke* (New Rochelle, NY: Arlington House, 1967), 213; Kirk, Ibid., 271, 63.
9. Kirk, Ibid., 8–9.
10. Birzer, Bradley J., *Russell Kirk American Conservative* (Lexington: University Press of Kentucky, 2015), 152.
11. Ibid., 273–274.
12. Ibid., 158–159.
13. Ibid., 156.

14. Scotchie, Joseph, ed., *Paleoconservatives* (New Brunswick, NJ: Transaction Publishers, 1999), 61, 65, 76–77.

15. Wills, Gary, *Reagan's America* (New York: Doubleday and Company, 1987), 381–382.

16. Kristol, Irving, *Two Cheers for Capitalism* (New York: Basic Books, 1978), 66–67, 262; Bell, Daniel, *The Cultural Contradictions of Capitalism* (New York: Basic Books, 1976), 70–76, 277.

17. Will, George, F., *The Woven Figure* (New York: Scribner, 1997), 81; Will, George F., *The Pursuit of Virtue and Other Tory Notions* (New York: Simon and Schuster, 1982), 36–38, 45.

18. Hart, Jeffrey, *The Making of the American Conservative Mind National Review and Its Times* (Wilmington, DE: ISI Books, 2005), 306, 361–363.

19. Pope John XXIII, *Mater et Magistra* (New York: America Press, 1961), 22–39; Judis, John B., *William F. Buckley, Jr.* (New York: Simon and Schuster, 1988), 186.

20. Buckley, William F., *Let Us Talk of Many Things* (New York: Basic Books, 2008), 232–232.

21. Burns, Jennifer, *Goddess of the Market* (New York: Oxford University Press, 2009), 42–43.

22. Judis, *William F. Buckley, Jr.*, 161.

23. Nozick, Robert, *Anarchy, State, and Utopia* (New York: Basic Books, 1974), ix.

24. Meyer, Frank S., *In Defense of Freedom and Related Essays* (Indianapolis: Liberty Fund, 1996) 13, 29; Buckley, William F., Jr., ed., *American Conservative Thought in the Twentieth Century* (Indianapolis: Bobs–Merrill Company, 1970), 85f.

25. Friedman, Milton, *Capitalism and Freedom* (Chicago: University of Chicago Press, 1982), 133; Foner, Eric, *The Story of American Freedom* (New York: W. W. Norton, 1998), 309.

26. Hayek, Friedrich A., *Road to Serfdom* (Chicago: University of Chicago Press, 1944), 38–39; Phillips-Fein, Kim, *Invisible Hands* (New York: W.W. Norton, 2009), 71; Nishiyama, Chiaki and Leube, Kurt R., *The Essence of Hayek* (Stanford: Hoover Institute Press, 1984), 285.

27. Von Mises, Ludwig, *Planning for Freedom* (South Holland, IL: Libertarian Press, 1962), 1, 17; Von Mises, Ludwig, *Economic Planning* (Indianapolis: Liberty Fund, 1979), 27–29; Von Mises, Ludwig, *The Free and Prosperous Commonwealth* (Princeton, NJ: Van Nostrand Co., 1962), 54.

28. Kristol, *Two Cheers*, 67–68; Kristol, Irving, *Neoconservatism: The Autobiography of an Idea* (New York: Free Press, 1995), 101–103.

29. Johnson, Haynes, *Sleepwalking through History* (New York: W. W. Norton, 1991), 198.

30. Kristol, Irving, *Reflections of a Neoconservative* (New York: Basic Books, 1983), 76: Kristol, Irving, "The Neoconservative Persuasion," *The Weekly Standard*, August 25, 2003; Hoeveler, J. David, Jr., *Watch on the Right Conservative Intellectuals in the Reagan Era* (Madison: University of Wisconsin Press, 1991), 98–99, 277.

31. Novak, Michael, *The American Vision* (Washington: American Enterprise, 1978), 9; Novak, Michael, *Toward a Theology of the Corporation* (Washington: American Enterprise Institute, 1981), 39.

32. Micklethwait, John and Woolridge, Adrian, *The Right Nation* (New York: The Penguin Press, 2004), 80; Weidenbaum, Murray, *The Competition of Ideas* (New Brunswick, NJ: Transaction Publishers, 2009), 23, 31.

33. Allison, John A., *The Financial Crisis and the Free Market Cure* (New York: McGraw Hill, 2013), 253–254.

34. Bellant, Russ, *The Coors Connection* (Boston: South End Press, 1991), xv, 1; Lind, Michael, *Up from Conservatism* (New York: Free Press, 1996), 87; O'Connor, Mike, *A Commercial Republic* (Lawrence: University of Kansas Press, 2014), 206.

35. Schaller, Michael, *Right Turn* (New York: Oxford University Press, 2007), 34–35.

36. Rossiter, *Conservatism in America*, 201, 202–203.

CHAPTER 6

1. Shermer, Elizabeth Tandy, ed., *Barry Goldwater and the Remaking of the American Political Landscape* (Tucson: University of Arizona Press, 2013), 3–4.

2. Goldwater, Barry, *The Conscience of a Conservative* (New York: Hillman Books, 1960), 21, 23–24, 35–37, 60–64.

3. Goldberg, Robert Alan, *Barry Goldwater* (New Haven: Yale University Press, 1995), 301, 331.

4. Goldwater, Barry, *The Coming Breaking Point* (New York: Macmillan Publishing, 1976), passim.

5. Evans, Thomas W., *The Education of Ronald Reagan* (New York: Columbia University Press, 2006), 238–249.

6. Johnson, Haynes, *Sleepwalking through History* (New York: W. W. Norton, 1991), 72, 74.

7. Selvidge, Marla J., *Fundamentalism Today* (Elgin, IL: Brethren Press, 1984), 58.

8. Stockman, David A., *The Triumph of Politics* (New York: Harper & Row, 1986), 382, 395; *New York Times*, July 10, 1985, 14; Johnson, *Sleepwalking through History*, 110–111.

9. Gilder, George, *Recapturing the Spirit of Enterprise* (San Francisco: ICS Press, 1992), 307–308; Gilder, George, *Wealth and Poverty* (New York: Basic Books, 1981), x, 45, 68, 191.

10. Lind, Michael, *Up from Conservatism* (New York: Free Press, 1996), 4.

CHAPTER 7

1. Foley, Elizabeth Price, *The Tea Party* (New York: Cambridge University Press, 2012), 225, 227.

2. Dimaggio, Anthony R., *The Rise of the Tea Party* (New York: Monthly Review Press, 2011), 10, 13; Leahy, Michael Patrick, *Covenant of Liberty: The Ideological Origins of the Tea Party Movement* (New York: Broadside Books, 2012), 248–250.

3. Armey, Dick and Kibbe, Matt, *Give Us Liberty* (New York: William Morrow, 2010), 171.

Sources

Adams, Henry, *The Education of Henry Adams*. New York: Random House, 1931.

Allison, John A., *The Financial Crisis and the Free Market Cure*. New York: McGraw Hill, 2013.

Armey, Dick and Kibbe, Matt, *Give Us Liberty*. New York: William Morrow, 2010.

Ayling, Stanley, *Edmund Burke: His Life and Opinions*. New York: St. Martin's Press, 1988.

Bell, Daniel, *The Cultural Contradictions of Capitalism*. New York: Basic Books, 1976.

Bell, Daniel and Kristol, Irving, eds., *Capitalism Today*. New York: Basic Books, 1970.

Beth, Loren, *The Development of the American Constitution*. New York: Harper & Row, 1971.

Birzer, Bradley J., *Russell Kirk American Conservative*. Lexington: University Press of Kentucky, 2015.

Bryfonski, Dedria, *The Banking Crisis*. Detroit: Greenhaven Press, 2010.

Buckley, William F., Jr., *Let Us Talk of Many Things*. New York: Basic Books, 2008.

Burke, Edmund, *Reflections on the Revolutions in France*. New York: Oxford University Press, 1993.

Burns, Jennifer, *Goddess of the Market: Ayn Rand and the American Right*. New York: Oxford University Press, 2009.

Canavan, Francis P., *The Political Reason of Edmund Burke*. Durham, NC: Duke University Press, 1960.

Commager, Henry Steele, *The American Mind*. New Haven: Yale University Press, 1959.

Cone, Carl B., *Burke on the Nature of Politics*. n.p.: University of Kentucky Press, 1964.

Conwell, Russell H., *Acres of Diamonds*. New York: Harper & Brothers, 1915.

Crowe, Ian, ed., *The Enduring Edmund Burke*. Wilmington, DE: Intercollegiate Studies Institute, 1997.

Current, Richard N., *Daniel Webster and the Rise of National Conservatism*. Boston: Little Brown and Company, 1955.

Den Uyl, Douglas J. and Rasmussen, Douglas B., eds., *The Philosophic Thought of Ayn Rand*. Urbana: University of Illinois Press, 1984.

Dimaggio, Anthony R., *The Rise of the Tea Party*. New York: Monthly Review Press, 2011.

Donovan, Timothy Paul, *Henry and Brooks Adams*. Norman: University of Oklahoma Press, 1961.

Dorrien, Gary J., *The Neoconservative Mind*. Philadelphia: Temple University Press, 1993.

Duffy, Michael and Goodgame, Dan, *Marching in Place*. New York: Simon and Schuster, 1992.

Easton, Nina J., *The Gang of Five*. New York: Simon and Schuster, 2000.

Elkins, Stanley and McKitrick, Eric, *The Age of Federalism*. New York: Oxford University Press, 1993.

Evans, Thomas W., *The Education of Ronald Reagan*. New York: Columbia University Press, 2006.

Federici, Michael P., *The Political Philosophy of Alexander Hamilton*. Baltimore: Johns Hopkins University Press, 2012.

Feldman, Stephen, *Neoconservative Politics and the Supreme Court*. New York: New York University Press, 2013.

Foley, Elizabeth Price, *The Tea Party*. New York: Cambridge University Press, 2012.

Foner, Eric, *The Story of American Freedom*. New York: W. W. Norton & Company, 1998.

Ford, Worthington Chauncey, ed., *Letters of Henry Adams 1892–1918*. Boston: Houghton Mifflin, 1938.

Freeman, Michael, *Edmund Burke and the Critique of Political Radicalism*. Chicago: University of Chicago Press, 1980.

Friedman, Milton, *Capitalism and Freedom*. Chicago: University of Chicago Press, 1982.

Gabriel, Ralph Henry, *The Course of American Democratic Thought*. New York: The Roland Press, 1940.

Genovese, Eugene, *The Southern Tradition*. Cambridge: Harvard University Press, 1994.

Gilder, George, *Recapturing the Spirit of Enterprise*. San Francisco: ICS Press, 1992.

Gilder, George, *Wealth and Poverty*. New York: Basic Books, 1981.

Goldberg, Robert Alan, *Barry Goldwater*. New Haven: Yale University Press, 1995.

Goldman, Eric F., *Rendezvous with Destiny*. New York: Vintage Books, 1956.

Goldwater, Barry, *The Coming Breaking Point*. New York: Macmillan Publishing, 1976.

Goldwater, Barry, *The Conscience of a Conservative*. New York: Hillman Books, 1960.

Harbour, William R., *The Foundations of Conservative Thought*. Notre Dame, IN: University of Notre Dame Press, 1982.

Hart, Jeffrey, *The Making of the American Conservative Mind*. Wilmington, DE: ISI Books, 2005.

Hayek, Friedrich A., *The Road to Serfdom*. Chicago: University of Chicago Press, 1944.

Herrera, R. A., *Orestes Brownson: Sign of Contradiction*. Wilmington, DE: ISI Books, 1999.

Hoeveler, J. David, Jr., *Watch on the Right Conservative Intellectuals in the Reagan Era*. Madison: University of Wisconsin Press, 1991.

Hofstadter, Richard, *The Paranoid Style of American Politics*. New York: Vintage Books, 1967.

Hofstadter, Richard, *Social Darwinism in American Thought*. Boston: Beacon Press, 1955.

Johnson, Haynes, *Sleepwalking through History*. New York: W. W. Norton & Company, 1991.

Judis, John B., *William F. Buckley, Jr*. New York: Simon and Schuster, 1988.

Kelly, Alfred H. and Harbison, Winfred A., *The American Constitution*. New York: W. W. Norton & Company, 1963.

Kennedy, David M., *Freedom from Fear*. New York: Oxford University Press, 1999.

Ker, Ian, *John Henry Newman*. New York: Oxford University Press, 1990.

Kirk, Russell, *The Conservative Mind*. Chicago: Regenery Books, 1986.

Kirk, Russell, *Edmund Burke: A Genius Reconsidered*. New Rochelle, NY: Arlington House, 1967.

Kristol, Irving, *Neoconservatives: The Autobiography of an Idea*. New York: Free Press, 1995.

Kristol, Irving, *Reflections of a Neoconservative*. New York: Basic Books, 1983.

Kristol, Irving, *Two Cheers for Capitalism*. New York: Basic Books, 1978.

Lash, Christopher, *The Culture of Narcissism*. New York: W. W. Norton and Company, 1979.

Leahy, Michael Patrick, *Covenant of Liberty: The Ideological Origins of the Tea Party Movement.* New York: Broadside Books, 2012.

Lerner, Max, *America as a Civilization.* New York: Simon and Schuster, 1957.

Leuchtenburg, William E., ed., *The New Deal.* New York: Harper & Row, 1968.

Lind, Michael, *Up from Conservatism.* New York: The Free Press, 1996.

Lively, Jack, trans., *The Works of Joseph de Maistre.* New York: The Macmillan Company, 1965.

Lora, Ronald, *Conservative Minds in America.* Chicago: Rand McNally, 1971.

Machlup, Fritz, ed., *Essays on Hayek.* New York: New York University Press, 1976.

Mansfield, Harvey C., Jr., ed., *Selected Letters of Edmund Burke.* Chicago: University of Chicago Press, 1984.

Martin, Brian, *John Henry Newman.* New York: Oxford University Press, 1982.

McClelland, J. S., *The French Right.* New York: Harper & Row, 1970.

McCloskey, Robert Green, *American Conservatism in the Age of Enterprise 1865–1910.* New York: Harper & Row, 1951.

McCullough, David, *John Adams.* New York: Simon and Schuster, 2001.

Medvetz, Thomas, *Think Tanks in America.* Chicago: University of Chicago Press, 2012.

Meyer, Frank, *In Defense of Freedom and Related Essays.* Indianapolis: Liberty Fund, 1996.

Meyer, Frank S., ed., *What Is Conservatism.* New York: Holt, Rinehart and Winston, 1964.

Micklethwait, John, *The Right Nation: Conservative Power in America.* New York: Penguin Press, 2004.

Miller, John C., *Alexander Hamilton and the Growth of the New Nation.* New York: Harper & Row, 1959.

Newman, John Henry, *The Idea of a University.* New Haven: Yale University Press, 1996.

Nishiyama, Chiaka and Leobe, Kurt, *The Essence of Hayek.* Stanford, CA: Hoover Institution Press, 1984.

Novak, Michael, *The American Vision.* Washington: American Enterprise Institute, 1978.

Novak, Michael, *Capitalism and Socialism a Theological Inquiry.* Washington: American Enterprise Institute, 1979.

Novak, Michael, *Toward a Theology of the Corporation.* Washington: American Enterprise Institute, 1981.

Nozick, Robert, *Anarchy, State, and Utopia.* New York: Basic Books, 1974.

Oakeshott, Michael, *Rationalism in Politics.* New York Basic Books, 1962.

O'Connor, Mike, *A Commercial Republic.* Lawrence: University Press of Kansas, 2014.

Persons, Stow, ed., *Social Darwinism: Selected Essays of William Graham Sumner.* Englewood Cliffs, NJ: Prentice Hall, 1963.

Phillips-Fein, Kim, *Invisible Hands: The Making of the Conservative Movement from the New Deal to Reagan.* New York: W. W. Norton & Company, 2009.

Piketty, Thomas, *Capital in the Twenty-First Century.* Cambridge, MA: Belknap Press of Harvard University, 2014.

Reagan, Ronald, *An American Life.* New York: Simon and Schuster, 1990.

Robin, Corey, *The Reactionary Mind.* New York: Oxford University Press, 2011.

Rosenthal, Lawrence and Trost, Christine, eds., *Steep: The Precipitous Rise of the Tea Party.* Berkeley: University of California Press, 2012.

Rossiter, Clinton, *Conservatism in America.* New York: Vintage Books, 1962.

Schaller, Michael, *Right Turn.* New York: Oxford University Press, 2007.

Schlesinger, Arthur M., Jr., *The Age of Jackson.* Boston: Little Brown, 1953.

Scotchie, Joseph, ed., *The Paleoconservatives New Voices of the Old Right.* New Brunswick, NJ: Transaction Publishers, 1999.

Scruton, Roger, *The Meaning of Conservatism.* Totowa, NJ: Barnes and Noble Books, 1980.

Sellers, Charles, *The Market Revolution.* New York: Oxford University Press, 1991.

Selvidge, Marla J., *Fundamentalism Today.* Elgin, IL: Brethren Press, 1984.

Shermer, Elizabeth Tandy, ed., *Barry Goldwater and the Remaking of the American Political Landscape.* Tucson: University of Arizona Press, 2013.

Smith, Page, *John Adams,* vol. 2. Garden City, NY: Doubleday & Co., 1962.

Smith III, Ted J., ed., *In Defense of Tradition: Collected Shorter Writings of Richard M. Weaver, 1929–1963.* Indianapolis, IN: Liberty Fund, 2000.

Stanlis, Peter J., ed., *Edmund Burke Selected Writings and Speeches.* New Brunswick, NJ: Transaction Publishers, 2007.

Sternhell, Zeev, *The Anti-Enlightenment Tradition.* New Haven: Yale University Press, 2010.

Stevenson, Elizabeth, ed., *A Henry Adams Reader.* Garden City, NY: Doubleday & Co., 1958.

Stockman, David A., *The Triumph of Politics.* New York: Harper & Row, 1986.

Strahan, Randall, *Leading Representatives.* Baltimore: Johns Hopkins University Press, 2007.

Twelve Southerners, *I'll Take My Stand.* Baton Rouge: Louisiana State University Press, 1977.

Vaisse, Justin, *Neoconservatism*. Cambridge: Harvard University Press, 2010.

Viereck, Peter, *Conservatism: From John Adams to Churchill*. Princeton, NJ: Van Nostrand, 1956.

Viereck, Peter, *Conservatism Revisited*. New York: The Free Press, 1962.

Viguerie, Richard A., *Conservatives Betrayed*. Los Angeles: Basic Books, 2006.

Von Mises, Ludwig, *Economic Policy*. Indianapolis, IN: Liberty Fund, 1979.

Von Mises, Ludwig, *The Free and Prosperous Commonwealth*. Princeton, NJ: Van Nostrand, 1962.

Von Mises, Ludwig, *Planning for Freedom*. South Holland, IL: Libertarian Press, 1962.

Wall, Joseph Frazier, ed., *The Andrew Carnegie Reader*. Pittsburgh: University of Pittsburgh Press, 1992.

Waterhouse, Benjamin C., *Lobbying America*. Princeton: Princeton University Press, 2014.

Weaver, Richard M., *Ideas Have Consequences*. Chicago: University of Chicago Press, 1984.

Weidenbaum, Murray, *The Competition of Ideas: The World of Washington Think Tanks*. New Brunswick, NJ: Transaction Publishers, 2009.

Wilentz, Sean, *The Rise of American Democracy*. New York: W. W. Norton, 2005.

Will, George F., *The Pursuit of Virtue and Other Tory Notions*. New York: Simon and Schuster, 1982.

Will, George F., *The Woven Figure Conservatism and America's Fabric, 1994–1997*. New York: Scribner, 1997.

Wills, Gary, *Reagan's America*. New York: Doubleday & Co., 1987.

Wood, Gordon, *Empire of Liberty*. New York: Oxford University Press, 2009.

Index

ABOUT THE AUTHOR

MARIO R. DiNUNZIO is emeritus professor of history at Providence College in Rhode Island. His published works include Praeger's *Franklin D. Roosevelt and the Third American Revolution* as well as *American Democracy and the Authoritarian Tradition of the West, Theodore Roosevelt: An American Mind,* and *Woodrow Wilson: Essential Writings and Speeches of the Scholar-President.*